this is the
COLLIE

Ch. Beulah's Golden Mity Sol, owned by Mrs. N. K. George. Photo by C. M. Cooke.

by
ESTHER McCLOSKEY

Distributed in the U.S.A. by T.F.H. Publications, Inc., 211 West Sylvania Avenue, P.O. Box 27, Neptune City, N.J. 07753; in England by T.F.H. (Gt. Britain) Ltd., 13 Nutley Lane, Reigate, Surrey; in Canada to the book store and library trade by Clarke, Irwin & Company, Clarwin House, 791 St. Clair Avenue West, Toronto 10, Ontario; in Canada to the pet trade by Rolf C. Hagen Ltd., 3225 Sartelon Street, Montreal 382, Quebec; in Southeast Asia by Y.W. Ong, 9 Lorong 36 Geylang, Singapore 14; in Australia and the south Pacific by Pet Imports Pty. Ltd., P.O. Box 149, Brookvale 2100, N.S.W., Australia. Published by T.F.H. Publications, Inc. Ltd., The British Crown Colony of Hong Kong.

To
Rudy Engle
and
Charles A. Wernsman

ISBN 0-87666-273-4

Contents

Photos by Louise Van Der Meid

Foreword

After many years of working with a breed, showing, breeding and studying it, one assumes that he has accumulated a great deal of knowledge and experience. It would seem that to write a book about that breed would be a simple matter of gathering and cataloguing this knowledge, then putting it down on paper. This, I have found, is not so. What is learned, through study and observation over the years, is often filled with half-truths and empty spots.

To be completely objective in the search for truthful answers to every question was perhaps the most difficult hurdle to overcome.

Yes, writing this book was a chore, but I feel it was very much worth while. I now know how little I knew before; and in the light of new and continued knowledge and scientific research and application in the various phases of animal husbandry, genetics and medicine, I can appreciate how much there is yet to know. I think, from this experience, that no one can consider himself an authority on any subject until he has written a thorough and complete treatise on that subject.

All the exhaustive research, all that I know, have learned and borrowed from knowledgeable sources I pass on to you in this book, with the hope that you will use what you find here for the betterment of the grand breed we love, the Collie.

I.
Origin and History
—The Beginning

The story of the relationship between dog and man starts long before the beginnings of recorded history. Anthropologists tell us that dogs played a part in man's life as far back as the middle of the Paleolithic Era some five million years ago. This partnership between man and dog is a natural one, and the reasons for its beginning are as valid today as they were then. Primitive man found in the dog a beast which could be controlled, whose feral instincts could be fashioned to conform to his needs—an animal whose natural talents complimented his own. It was fleet where man was slow; it had a highly developed scenting ability, and its auditory sense was many times sharper than man's. The dog found and ran down game for man to kill and eat. It helped fight off marauding beasts of prey. In return, man protected his dog from the larger carnivores, gave him shelter and food and tended to his injuries.

And so a pact was formed between man and dog, a partnership that was to endure from the misty beginnings of time down to the present day. For in the dog man had found more than a hunter; he had found a friend, a companion and a guardian.

As man progressed out of ignorance into understanding, the time came when his role of hunter no longer suited him. In his wanderings he had found fair land on which he wished to stay and build permanent shelter. But always, to keep the bellies of his family filled, he had to travel in the wake of the wild herds. To end this precarious existence, he learned to trap and capture the vagrant food beasts, eliminating the constant need to hunt and ending the deadly periods of starvation that came when the herds disappeared. So began the pastoral age of man, and with this change in man's environment, a new use was born for his dog.

The author with three of her Collies.

Here we find the real beginning of a specialized breed. An animal evolved which could adapt itself to the herding and protection of its master's flocks, and the earliest shepherd breed was born. Within these early dogs mutations occurred, and when these sudden changes in heredity made the dog more adaptable to its work, man selected for them. By this natural process all the varied breeds of dogs came into being.

That shepherds and hounds were the earliest specialized breeds known to man is a definite fact. We cannot, however, be any more specific than that; for the truth is that the evolution of the herding dog which eventually came into focus in Scotland as the Collie is hidden in the years.

We know that during the 1800's Thomas Bewick carved a woodcut of the local Scottish working dogs. This woodcut unmistakingly depicts a rough-coated and a smooth-coated Collie, and the definite breed characteristics seen in the woodcut lead us to assume that the breed was already established in this area for at least a century.

To attempt to find a definite origin we must go back in history to the time when the Romans invaded the Scottish Isles and came as far North as the River Tay in 500 B.C. Mute testimony to this invasion is the wall built by the Romans in the Tay locale, the stones of which are still in evidence today. It is the author's belief that when the Romans came they brought their guard and hunting dogs with them, and these canines of the conquerors were bred to the local Scottish herding dogs to develop a new breed. With selection through the centuries these foundation animals became the sheepherding dogs of Scotland, the noble and lovely breed known today as the Collie.

The very origin of the breed name is open to speculation due to the many words from which various authorities claim that the name Collie was derived. The author's belief in the Roman-Scottish breed blending in ancient times can be substantiated to a certain extent by the Latin word *collaboro*, which could well be the original name of the Collie before time, alien interpretation and lingual difference slightly changed and shortened it. *Collaboro* means *to labor with or together*. This definition certainly fits the working Collie who labored with his master to keep the flocks together and free from harm. *Collatio*, meaning the putting together of possessions, is another word from which the breed name may be a derivative. Again we have a word that deftly describes the Collie's basic work. The word *Collis*, frequently used to identify the sheepherding dogs of the region in the 1800's means, when translated, the high ground or hills. With further interpretation we arrive at a designation of the dog of the high ground or the Scottish Highlands. To substantiate this assumption we know definitely that the Collie-type dog was the sheepherding dog of the Highlands. The simple proof of this is the fact that the Northern hills were the browsing land of the Scottish sheep and the lowlands were the coal mining or industrial area.

Shakespeare, describing the night, used the phrase "collied night", which has led many students of the breed to the belief that the original strains were black or dark in color, perhaps more closely resembling the modern tri-color than the other known color phases.

Speculation as to the basic color and name source of the breed can go on indefinitely, but this we do know: that the sheepherding dogs of the Scottish Highlands gradually, in the crucible of time and aided by natural selection to do their job, evolved into a breed type that was eventually to become the Collie. Different sections of the

The Collie has long been known as a friendly, trustworthy, affectionate dog. He is especially gentle with children and makes a very fine pet.

In the Scottish Highlands, as in many countries around the world, the Collie is a working dog and he usually works well with other animals, especially horses. There sometimes seems to be a natural love between a horse and a Collie and these animals seem to be annoyed at the photographer for interrupting their 'conversation'.

Highlands undoubtedly had varied types, but one thing these basic types had in common were ruggedness, intelligence, and general soundness.

Inevitably there must have come a time in the evolution of the breed when civilization took a hand in its fashioning. When civilization reached into the rural areas for the wool and meat, men came together to discuss crops and weather, flocks, prices, and finally to boast about their dogs. The natural evolutionary processes which formed a specific breed were then aided by some crude attempts at selective breeding. As the herding ability and intelligence of a particular dog was recognized, his fame would spread. Other herders would breed their bitches to him and select for the desired qualities of the sire from amongst the puppies. One highly regarded dog could, in this way, stamp his genetic qualities on many puppies. Gradually, greater structural and mental uniformity would thus be attained.

The early Collies were smaller animals than the present-day dogs, measuring approximately 14 inches at the shoulder. This was true of both the Smooth and the Rough. Thomas Bewick's woodcut shows the Smooth Collie with a short tail which was probably docked, but both Smooth and Rough in the woodcut are of like size, the Smooth shown possessing perhaps a bit more substance in body than the Rough. From the woodcut it is evident that the only basic differences lie in the variety of coat and, of course, the Smooth's docked tail.

THE SMOOTH COLLIE

The Smooth Collie was a drover dog whose job it was to drive sheep and cattle to market. Bewick claimed that the immediate ancestor of the Collie was the "ban-dog" which was a descendant of the basic dog breed, *Canis molossus*, a mastiff-type animal. Bewick also tells us that the Smooth was a larger, stronger and fiercer dog than the sheepherding or shepherd's dog of the day, the rough coated animal.

Early specimens displayed large areas of black in their coats, as did the sheepherding, rough coated dogs. Shakespeare's "collied night"

Ch. Hughley Hush Puppy Blue, owned by Miss M. J. Rhys. Photo by C. M. Cooke.

notwithstanding, both varieties were called "Coally Dogs" because, it was said, the black in their coats resembled the black coal mined in the lowlands. Stonehenge, in 1867, refers to the breed as the "Highland Sheepdog" and "Scotch Colley".

Although the Smooth variety was well known in all areas of Scotland, it is the opinion of practically all authorities that it was developed in the North of England and particularly in the county of Northumberland, the center for this coat variety of the Scotch shepherd. The black and white mottled colored Collie was definitely a Northumbrian strain, developed in this specific locale.

In dog shows in the early 1860's, the Rough and Smooth varieties were shown in the same classes and it was not until 1870, at the Darlington show, that the Smooth Collie was given a separate classification. Even then, the name "Collie" was not commonly used to designate the breed.

13

One of America's finest Collies, Ch. Bellhaven Bluestone.

The Smooth variety of Collie is judged by the same standard in dog shows as the Rough variety, but the Smooth has never achieved the general popularity that has come the way of his heavier coated brother.

THE ROUGH COLLIE

This majestic variety of the popular Collie is the sheepherding dog, working directly with the flocks, as opposed to the Smooth, whose job it was to drive both sheep and cattle to market. The Rough watched over and guarded his master's sheep at pasture, kept them bunched, brought in strays, helped move them to new pasture and generally performed superlatively the job for which sheepherding dogs had been bred to perform since man cast aside his spear for the shepherd's staff.

The earlier forms of the breed were, as I mentioned earlier, smaller than the present dogs. They also possessed a shorter and broader head and heavier ears and, though refinement had not yet taken place, they were of the basic Collie type. It was one of the first

Ch. Laund Liberation of Bellhaven, 89 times Best Collie, along with many Best in Groups and Best in Shows.

Ch. Bellhaven's Golden Sceptreson, sired by Ch. Southport Sceptre of Bellhaven. The dam was Ch. Bellhaven's Diadem's Diana.

breeds for which classes were provided in the early dog shows in England. The Collie was recognized as a breed and shown in its own classes at the Birmingham Dog Society Show in 1860.

The development of the grand Rough Collie of today is due to careful breeding and selection for wanted virtues and refinements. It was bred up to the desired modern size as early as 1886 and stood in the wings—a majestic, magnificently-coated, sagacious breed, waiting for the popularity it deserved. That acclaim came in the early '60's at Balmoral when England's beloved Queen Victoria saw specimens of the Rough Coated Collie and became enamored of the breed. Word of her enthusiasm for the Collie spread quickly and suddenly this grand breed found itself standing in the spotlight of popularity. From that day, when queenly choice pointed the finger of desirability at the Collie and brought it into focus, its popularity has never waned.

SMOOTH AND ROUGH ONE BREED?

This is a moot question. It is difficult to state, or find any reasonable authority to state, which was first—the Smooth or the Rough variety of Collie. Are they the same breed or did they have different beginnings? Some authorities claim that the two varieties did have different beginnings and were separate breeds. Others propose that they were the same breed in the beginning and coat-quality was selected for the job they were called upon to do, the rough-coated dogs for herding, the smoother-coated dogs for driving. It is a fact that, with few exceptions, most sheepherding breeds do have rough coats.

It could also be that, in the early formation of the breed, the different coat qualities mirrored the varied coats of their early ancestors. Then too, perhaps a mutation may have occurred within the structure of the one sheepherding breed that produced a different kind of coat than was generally known and that some breeders, seeing value in that mutant coat, bred for it. Natural selection could also account for the difference in coat, coupled with environment, so that the conditions that contributed to the better, heavier, denser type of sheep's wool had their effect upon the coat of the dogs that herded the sheep.

That Roughs and Smooths were interbred we do know and they produced both coat varieties in the same litter. Even today an oc-

A magnificent headstudy of Can. Ch. Sandamac's Sandonna, C.D., litter sister of Sandaman. Sire: Can. Ch. Alandale Academy Award. Dam: Sanda Mac. Breeder-owner:
Edward and Mildred Horton.

Ch. Bellhaven's Blue Diadem.

casional Smooth makes its appearance in a litter of Roughs even though the pedigree shows nothing but Roughs as far back as it can be traced. The same is true in reverse, of Smooth breeding. This occurs even though, for almost a century, the coat varieties have not been interbred.

THE COLLIE IN AMERICA

In Colonial days in America, many of the early settlers and frontiersmen brought their dogs with them from England and Scotland, most of them being Collies. They were used to herd their masters' herbivorous animals, just as on their native heath. They were also used extensively to guard the property, possessions, and family of the settler. The land was not fenced; and these early dogs were worth their weight in gold as sentries, giving the alarm to ward off both four and two-legged marauders.

The American Kennel Club Stud Book of 1885 carries the first registrations of the breed, and many of the animals registered then were American bred, thus proving that the popularity of the Collie in America went back at least five to ten years. By the end of the nineteenth century there were already many kennels in this country specializing in Collies.

Since those early Colonial days, America has taken the Collie to its heart and the breed has flourished. This popularity had been given added incentive in the 1920's by a man of considerable stature, the late Albert Payson Terhune. At his Sunnybank Kennels he bred, loved and truly understood his great strain of Collies. But, what was more important to the breed, this gifted man wrote about his Collies with insight and rare literary charm. His novels became extremely popular and boosted the stock of this grand breed he loved so much. I remember that Mr. Terhune would not ship a dog to a purchaser. If you wished to buy one of his Collies you had to appear personally at his kennels and he would help to select *the* dog for you. If Mr. Terhune felt that you were not the proper kind of person to own one of his beloved animals, you would have to go elsewhere to buy. Undoubtedly Albert Payson Terhune immortalized the breed through his delightful stories about his Sunnybank dogs, as only a creative man could.

IMPORTANT STRAINS

The source of most of the fine Collie heritage in this country was Champion Magnet. From this one dog, bred and born in England, there flowed a rich river of genetic material that has formed type in this country to the present day.

Magnet was born in England in 1912 and later was imported to the United States. He was a twenty-four inch, sixty-two pound male who possessed correct size, type, balance, expression and true Collie character and temperament. A magnificent specimen, he was the equal of any of the present-day Collies.

Due to his many virtues, Magnet was used extensively at stud in this country and, being a dominant sire who gave much of his fine genetic heritage to his offspring, he became the source material that helped to establish many of the leading kennels and strains.

Some of the important strains he founded are Arken, Alstead, Arthea, Burnbrae, Honeybrook, Parader, Silver Ho, Tokalon, Poplar and Sterling. Magnet's son, Ch. Poplar Perfection, is also the foundation source of many of the best strains. Perfection's son, Ch. Eden Emerald, was another quality producer in the lines founded by his grandsire.

The great qualities of those magnificent animals that came down through the Magnet line have given us an array of fine individuals with which to carry on the important genetic lines within the breed and to keep our Collies the truly wonderful breed that they were meant to be.

One of the great early Collie lines came from a famous English sire, Charlemagne. The famous Ch. Christopher, imported to this country by Mitchel Harrison, of Chestnut Hill Kennel fame, was a great-great grandson of Charlemagne. From the sons of Christopher descended the modern Collie. Eclipse, a son of Christopher, was, in his time, one of the finest show dogs in England. Another "great" who came from the Christopher line was Ormskirk Emerald, called by some authorities the greatest Collie of his time.

In Britain, some of the people who furthered the breed can be known for the prefixes they used for the names of their Collies, names that are important in pedigree studies and known to all Collie fanciers. Among them we find: Southport, Wishaw, Woodman-sterne, Ormskirk, Billesley, Wellesbourne, Laund, Eden, Egbaston, Parbold, Ellwyn and Seedley, kennel prefixes to reckon with in tracing the lineage of fine Collies.

There were rumors, in those developmental days, of a cross of Borzoi into the breed to quickly narrow the heads, whispers of the "Russian" influence. But there is really no basic proof that this out-cross did occur, or if, by selection, the breeders arrived at the narrower head within the structure of the breed.

In America, two prominent men became Collie fanciers, J. Pierpont Morgan, the elder, and Samuel Untermyer. Both these men of wealth could and did purchase some of the finest Collies available in England and so advanced the breed in America enormously. Other winning exhibitors were J. I. Behling of Milwaukee, the Alstead Kennels of Mrs. C. M. Lunt, William Ellery's Val Verde Kennels, the Hungerford "Mountaineer" dogs, the Imna Kennels of Miss Bullock and, about 1904, Mr. and Mrs. E. C. Rand's Brae Brook Kennels in California.

As the 1900's progressed, new and important names came into being in the Collie fancy. Dr. O. P. Bennett established his Tazewell Kennels, and Edward L. Pickhardt, an avid student of the breed and still active as a judge today, brought into being his famous Sterling Kennels. Hertzville, Knocklayde, Lunt, Ilch, and Van Dyck are names that are at the very backbone of the breed. Mrs.

Headstudy of Kitsap's Hi Jac, now in the Netherlands. Sire: American and Canadian Ch. Sandamac's Mr. Sandaman. Dam: Collevoy's Kit-N-Kaboodle. Breeder: Frances Whitlock.

Ilch's Bellhaven Kennels at Red Bank, New Jersey, has produced some of the greatest Collies of the decade. One of her dogs, Bellhaven Black Lucason, has one of the greatest winning show records of all American-bred Collies. Other Collie establishments are the St. Adrian Kennels and the Noranda Kennels of Mr. and Mrs. Long, Jr.

Perhaps the oldest and finest strain of Collies in America is that of the Arken Kennels, owned by the late Charles A. Wernsman of Connecticut. Charlie and his wife Lillian were old friends of the author, and it was Charlie who advised and aided me in the breed. His knowledge was endless; no finer tutor could be found anywhere.

Ch. Bellhaven's Enchanter. Sire: Ch. Bellhaven's Black Lance. Dam: Ch. Bellhaven's Enchanting.

I know all Collie breeders and authorities will agree with me when I say that the value of the Arken dogs was so great that it is beyond estimation. From Arken breeding come many of the greatest of our present-day winners.

Type has changed since the early dogs of the breed and, even though Magnet and the great strains that he gave us set type for the Collie, change is constant. It is a part of progress and of life. However, this must be upward toward greater merit and perfection or it brings us retrogression. The pattern of heredity must be clearly seen and understood if progress is to be made in breeding activity. That pattern cannot be known unless it is unveiled, and the faults as well as the virtues evaluated.

In the light of modern-day knowledge of genetics, the breeding of fine dogs has not advanced as rapidly as it should have. Too many breeders lack the necessary knowledge and understanding of basic genetics. Too many others give it only lip service and run to the latest champion to breed, without ascertaining whether or not the dog is a fit mate, genetically, for their bitch. In the next chapter you will find an easy road to the wonderful world of genetics, a road that you can understand and use for the improvement of your stock. In the chapter that follows, The Riddle Of Inheritance, you will become acquainted with the various ways in which you can utilize this knowledge of inheritance.

2.

The Riddle of Inheritance

Before we begin to delve into the riddle of inheritance, we must first clear away the debris of old untruths and superstition so that we may see clearly the true structure that lies beyond. The inheritance of acquired characteristics is one of the fallacious theories that was widely believed and has its disciples even today. Birthmarking is another false theory which must be discarded in the light of present-day genetical knowledge. The genes which give our dogs all their inheritable material are isolated in the body from any environmental influence. What the host does or has done to him influences them not at all. The so-called "proofs" advanced by the adherents of both these bogus theories were simply isolated coincidences.

Telegony is another of the untrue beliefs about influencing inherited characteristics. This is the theory that the sire of one litter could or would influence the progeny of a future litter out of the same bitch but sired by an entirely different stud. Telegony is, in its essence, comparable to the theory of saturation. This is the belief that if a bitch is bred many times in succession to the same stud, she will become so "saturated" with his "blood" that she will produce only puppies of his type, even when mated to an entirely different stud. By far the strongest and most widely believed was the theory that the blood was the vehicle through which all inheritable material was passed from parents to offspring from one generation to the next. The taint of that superstition still persists in the phraseology we employ in our breeding terms such as "bloodlines," "percentage of blood," "pure-blooded," "blue-blooded," etc. This "blood" reference with regard to heredity crops up in all places and for all allied references, as witness the politician who cries vehemently, "I am proud that the blood of Paul Revere runs in my veins!" To achieve such a remarkable accomplishment would require transfusion from a long-dead corpse.

The truth was found in spite of such a persistent theory, and in the history of science there is no more dramatic story than that of the discovery of the true method of inheritance. No, the truth was not arrived at in some fine, endowed scientific laboratory gleaming with the mysterious implements of research. The scene was, instead, a small dirt garden in Moravia, which is now a part of Czechoslovakia. Here Johann Gregor Mendel, a monk, planted and crossed several varieties of common garden peas and quietly recorded the differences that occurred through several generations. Over a period of eight years this remarkable man continued his studies. Then, in 1865, he read a paper he had prepared with regard to his experiments to the local Brunn, a society of historians and naturalists. The society subsequently published this paper in its journal, which was obscure and definitely limited in distribution.

Now we come to the amazing part of this story. Mendel's theory of inheritance, which contained the fundamental laws upon which all modern advances in genetics have been based, gathered dust for thirty-four years, and it seemed that one of the most important scientific discoveries of the nineteenth century was to be lost to mankind. Then in 1900, sixteen years after Mendel's death, the paper was rediscovered and his great work given to the world.

Alstead Ablaza a noble son of Ch. El Troubadour of Arken.

The long coat of a Collie has been developed through an application of Mendelian principles. This is King O Dunrobin owned by Mrs. Lillian Driggs. The snow and cold helps develop a thick, healthy coat. Collies are outdoor dogs; give them plenty of opportunity to roam.

In his experiments with the breeding of garden peas, Mendel discovered and identified the units of heredity. He found that when two individual plants which differed in a unit trait were mated, one trait appeared in the offspring and one did not. The trait which was visible he named the "dominant" trait, and the one which was not visible he called the "recessive" trait. He proposed that traits, such as color, are transmitted by means of units in the sex cells and that one of these units must be pure, let us say either black or white, but never be a mixture of both. From a black parent which is pure for that trait, only black units are transmitted, and from a white

MENDELIAN EXPECTATION CHART

The six possible ways in which a pair of determiners can unite. Ratios apply to expectancy over large numbers of Collies, except lines nos. 1, 2 and 6 where exact expectancy is realized in every Collie litter.

parent, only white units can be passed down. However, when one parent is black and one is white, a hybrid occurs which transmits both the black and white units in equal amounts. The hybrid itself will take the color of the dominant parent, yet carry the other color as a recessive. Various combinations of unit crosses were tried by Mendel, and he found that there were six possible ways in which a pair of determiners (Mendel's "units") could combine with a similar pair. The chart above shows how this law of Mendel's operates and the expected results. This simple Mendelian law holds true in the actual breeding of all living things—of plants, mice, humans, or dogs.

The beginning of new life in animals arises from the union of a male sperm and a female egg cell during the process of breeding. Each sperm cell has a nucleus containing one set of chromosomes, which are small packages, or units, of inheritable material. Each egg also possesses a nucleus of one set of chromosomes. The new life formed by the union of sperm cell and egg cell then possesses two sets of chromosomes—one from the sperm, one from the egg, or one set from the sire and one set from the dam. When the sperm cell enters the egg, it does two things—it starts the development of the egg and it adds a set of chromosomes to the set already in the egg. Here is the secret of heredity, because in the chromosomes lie the living genes that shape the destiny of the unborn young. Thus we see that the pattern of physical and mental heredity is transmitted to our dog from its sire and dam through tiny living cells called genes, which are the connecting links between the puppy and his ancestors.

These packets of genes, the chromosomes, resemble long, paired strings of beads. Each pair is alike; the partners formed are the same, yet differ from the like partners of the next pair. In the male we find the exception to this rule, for here there is one pair of chromosomes composed of two that are not alike. These are the sex chromosomes, and in the male they are different from the female in that the female possesses a like pair while the male does not. If we designate the female chromosomes as x, then the female pair is $x x$. The male too has an x chromosome, but its partner is a y chromosome. If the male x chromosome unites with the female x chromosome, then the resulting embryo will be a female, but if the male y chromosome is carried by the particular sperm that fertilizes the female egg, the resulting progeny will be a male. It is, therefore, a matter of chance as to what sex the offspring will be, since sperm are capricious and fertilization is random.

The actual embryonic growth of the puppy is a process of division of cells to form more and more new cells, and at each cell division of the fertilized egg each of the two sets of chromosomes provided by sire and dam also divides, until all the myriad divisions of cells and chromosomes have reached an amount necessary to form a complete and living entity. Then birth becomes an accomplished fact, and we see before us a living, squealing Collie puppy.

What is he like, this puppy? He is what his controlling genes have made him. His sire and dam have contributed one gene of each kind to their puppy, and this gene which they have given him is but one of the two which each parent possesses for a particular characteristic. Since he has drawn these determiners at random, they can be either dominant or recessive genes. We can see his dominant heritage when he develops, but what he possesses in recessive traits is hidden.

]((((())))))((((((((((

Above, left: Chromosomes in the nucleus of a cell. Above, right: Chromosomes arranged in pairs, showing partnership.

There are rules governing dominant and recessive traits that are useful in summarizing what is known of the subject at the present time. We can be reasonably sure that a dominant trait: (1) does not skip a generation, (2) will affect a relatively large number of the progeny, (3) will be carried only by the affected individuals, (4) will minimize the danger of continuing undesirable characteristics in a strain, (5) will make the breeding formula of each individual quite certain.

With recessive traits we note that: (1) the trait may skip one or more generations, (2) on the average a relatively small percentage of the individuals in the strain carry the trait, (3) only those individuals which carry a pair of determiners for the trait exhibit it, (4) individuals carrying only one determiner can be ascertained only by mating, (5) the trait must come through both sire and dam.

You will hear some breeders say that the bitch contributes 60 per cent or more to the excellence of the puppies. Others swear that the influence of the sire is greater than that of the dam. Actually, the puppy receives 50 per cent of his germ plasm from each, though one parent may be so dominant that it seems that the puppy received most of his inheritable material from that parent. From the fact that the puppy's parents also both received but one set of determiners from each of their parents and in turn have passed on but one of their sets to the puppy, it would seem that one of those sets contributed by the grandparents has been lost and that therefore the puppy has inherited the germ plasm from only two of its grandparents, not four. Yet chromosomes cross over, and it is possible for the puppy's four grandparents to contribute an equal 25 per cent of all the genes inherited, or various and individual percentages, one grandparent contributing more and another less. It is even possible for the pup to inherit no genes at all from one grandparent and 50 per cent from another.

The genes that have fashioned this puppy of ours are of chemical composition and are living cells securely isolated from any outside influence, a point which we have made before and which bears repeating. Only certain kinds of man-directed radiation, some poisons or other unnatural means can cause change in the genes. No natural means can influence them. Environment can effect an individual but not his germ plasm. For instance, if the puppy's nutritional needs are not fully provided for during his period of growth, his end potential will not be attained; but, regardless of his outward appearance, his germ plasm remains inviolate and capable of passing on to the next generation the potential that was denied him by improper feeding.

Breeding fine Collies would be a simple procedure if all characteristics were governed by simple Mendelian factors, but, alas, this is not so. Single genes are not solely responsible for single characteristics, mental or physical. The complexity of any part of the body and its dependence upon other parts in order to function properly makes it obvious that we must deal with interlocking blocks of controlling genes in a life pattern of chain reaction. Eye color, for instance, is determined by a simple genetic factor, but the ability to see, the complicated mechanism of the eye, the nerves, the blood supply, the retina and iris, even your Collie's reaction to what he sees, are all part of the genetic pattern of which eye color is but a segment.

Since they are living cells in themselves, the genes can and do change or mutate. In fact, it is now thought that many more gene mutations take place than were formerly suspected, but that the great majority are either within the animal, where they cannot be seen, or are so small in general scope that they are overlooked. The dramatic mutations which affect the surface are the ones we notice and select for or against according to whether they direct us toward our goal or away from it. Again, with the vagary inherent in all living things, the mutated gene can change once again back to its original form.

Extreme examples of mutations are the albino, pure white and with pink eyes and nose, and the pure black. A male and female albino when bred together cannot produce any but albino young. When two pure mutant blacks are bred, they can produce only black young.

We see then that the Collie puppy is the product of his germ plasm, which has been handed down from generation to generation. We know that there are certain rules that generally govern the pattern formed by the genes and that a gene which prevents another gene from showing in an individual is said to be a dominant and the repressed gene a recessive. Remember, the animal itself is not dominant or recessive in color or any other characteristic. It is the gene that is dominant or recessive, as judged by results. We find that an animal can contain in each of his body cells a dominant and a recessive gene. When this occurs, the dog is said to be heterozygous. As illustrated in the Mendelian Expectation Chart, we know that there is an opposite to the heterozygous individual, an animal which contains two genes of the same kind in its cells—either two dominants or two recessives—and this animal is said to be homozygous. The loss of a gene or the gain of a gene, or the process of change among the genes, is known as mutation, and the animal affected is called a mutant.

Every bitch that stands before us, every stud we intend to use, is not just one dog, but two. Every living thing is a Jekyll and Hyde,

Ch. Bellhaven's Diadem's Diana. Sire: Ch. Eden Diadem of Bellhaven. Dam: Eng. Ch. Laund Blue Iris of Bellhaven.

ough changes in function and

n as men of science delve deeper
/hat we know today of inheritance
1 animal breeding, removing a great
ur operations. Yet we do not know
of top stock a cut-and-dried matter, or
pure science, with a definite answer to
iis is where the fascination lies. Life is
ies unstable, so that even with the greater
e will no doubt bring, it is possible that the
s will still remain a combination of science
of necessary genius and aesthetic innovation,
n to this riddle of inheritance.

ig. Sire: Ch. Bellhaven's Golden Sceptreson. Dam: Ch. Bellhaven's
At Last.

Ch. Lowerpark Blue

shadow and
breathes and
manifestatio
ment—the
yet this sh
see. This
genes—t
but the
for bot
to con
any p
accom
into t
becon
the d
us is
hered

33

Can Ch. Sandamac's Tony O'Tawnygold. Sire: American and Canadian Ch. Sandamac's Mr. Sandaman. Dam: To Kin Tawny. Breeder: Mrs. A. E. Deering. Owner: Edward and Mildred Horton.

Tawnygold Sandusky, C.D. Sire: American and Canadian Ch. Sandamac's Mr. Sandaman. Dam: To Kin Tawny Feather. Owned by Mrs. Gordon Brunswick.

3.
The Roots of Breeding

In today's mechanistic world, with its rushing pace and easy pleasures, much of the creative urge in man has been throttled. We who breed dogs are extremely fortunate, for in our work we have a real creative outlet—we are in the position of being able to mold beauty and utility in living flesh and blood. Our tools are the genes of inheritance, and our art, their infinite combination. We have the power to create a work of art that will show the evidence of our touch for generations to come.

Now that we have absorbed some of the basic facts of heredity, we can with greater understanding examine the various kinds of breeding which can be used in perpetuating wanted characteristics. We have learned that within the design of the germ plasm great variation occurs but within the breed itself as a whole, we have an average, or norm, which the great majority of dogs mirror. Draw a straight horizontal line on a piece of paper and label this line "norm." Above this line draw another and label it "above norm." This latter line represents the top dogs, the great ones, and the length of this line will be very much shorter than the length of the "norm" line. Below the "norm" line draw still another line, designating this to be "below norm." These are the animals possessing faults which we do not wish to perpetuate.

Since the time of the first registered Collies, the number of breeders who have molded the characteristics of the breed have been legion. So many have bred without a basic knowledge of any of the fundamentals that the stock produced has the detrimental effect of dangerously lowering the norm. Examine the pedigrees of your dogs, and in many instances you will find an example of this—a line incorporated in your pedigree that causes worry to the true student of breeding. The real objective of all breeding is to raise the norm of a given breed and thereby approach always closer to the breed standard.

Ch. Bellhaven's Liberation's Leone.

If we are to achieve the greatest good from any program of breeding, there are four important traits which we must examine. It is essential that these traits should never depart from the norm.

The first is fertility. The lack of this essential in any degree must be guarded against diligently.

The second is vigor. Loss of vigor, or hardiness, and its allied ills, such as lowered resistance to disease, finicky eating, etc., will lead to disaster.

Longevity is the third important trait. An individual of great worth—who represents a fortunate combination of excellent characteristics which he dominantly passes on to his offspring—must be useful for a long time after his or her worth is recognized by the progeny produced.

The fourth is temperament. Here is the sum total of the dog's usefulness to man in the various categories in which he serves. Lack of true Collie character nullifies any other advances which you may make in your breeding program.

The norm can be likened to the force of gravity, possessing a powerful pull toward itself, so that regression toward the average is strong, even though you have used in your breeding parents which are both above average. The same holds true for progeny bred from animals below norm, but from these you will get a lesser number which reach the mean average and a greater number which remain below norm. In the case of the better-than-average parents, some of the progeny will stay above the norm line and the majority will regress. Occasionally a dog of superior structure is produced by a poor family, but inevitably this animal is useless as a stud because he will produce all his objectionable family traits and none of the fortuitous characteristics he displays in himself. From a breeding standpoint it is far better to use an average individual from top stock than a top individual from average or below-average stock. It is also true that many times a great show dog produces average progeny while his little-known brother, obscured by the shadow of the great dog's eminence, produces many above-average young. This is not as strange as it sounds when we consider the fact that the individual animal is the custodian of his germ plasm and it is this germ plasm, not the individual, that produces. In this instance, due to variation in the germ plasm, the top dog does not possess the happy genetic

Ch. Wee Park's Mister Carrigan. Sire: Ch. Arrowhill Oklahoma Redman. Dam: Wee Parks Miss Topper. Breeder-owner: Mrs. R. C. Sugden.

Ch. Hell's Own Angel from Ugony, owned by Miss D. M. Young. Photo by C. M. Cooke.

combinations that his average brother does and so cannot produce stock of comparative value.

Any of the various categories of breeding practice which we will outline can be followed for the betterment of the breed if used intelligently. Regardless of which practice one follows, there generally comes a time when it is necessary to incorporate one or more of the other forms into the breeding program in order to concentrate certain genetic characters, or to introduce new ones which are imperative for over-all balance. Outcross breeding is not recommended as a consistent practice. Rather, it is a valuable adjunct to the other methods when used as a corrective measure. Yet outcross breeding in the Collie does not, as would be supposed from definition, produce completely heterozygous young. The root stock of the breed is the same regardless of which breeding partners are used, and much of the stock which represents what we term outcross breeding shows some common ancestry within a few generations.

INBREEDING

By breeding father to daughter, half brother to half sister, son to mother, and, by closest inbreeding of all, brother to sister, stability and purity of inherited material is obtained. Specifically, inbreeding concentrates both good features and faults, strengthening dominants and bringing recessives out into the open where they can be seen and evaluated. It supplies the breeder with the only control he can have over prepotency and homozygosity, or the combining and balancing of similar genetic factors. Inbreeding does not produce degeneration, it merely concentrates weaknesses already present so that they can be recognized and eliminated. This applies to both physical and psychical hereditary transmission.

The most important phases of inbreeding are: (1) to choose as nearly faultless partners as is possible; (2) to cull, or select, rigidly from the resultant progeny.

Selection is always important regardless of which breeding procedure is used, but in inbreeding it becomes imperative. It is of interest to note that the most successful inbreeding programs have used as a base an animal which was either inbred or line-bred. To

Ch. Bellhaven's Son O'Black Lucason.

the breeder, the inbred animal represents an individual whose breeding formula has been so simplified that certain results can almost always be depended upon.

There are many examples of extreme inbreeding over a period of generations in other animal and plant life. Perhaps the most widely known are the experimental rats bred by Dr. Helen L. King, which are the result of over one hundred generations of direct brother and sister mating. The end result has been bigger, finer rodents than the original pair, and entirely dependable uniformity. Dr. Leon F. Whitney has bred and developed a beautiful strain of tropical fish, *Lebistes reticulatus*, commonly known as "guppies," by consecutive brother to sister breeding for ten generations. Dr. Whitney found that each succeeding generation was a little smaller and less vigorous, but that in the fifth generation a change occurred for the better, and in each generation thereafter size, vigor, and color improved. This pattern should hold true with all life forms developed from the same type of breeding.

Ch. Conrad's Dancing in the Dark, bred and owned by Roy L. Ayers, Sr.

It is interesting to note that genetic experiments with plants, vegetables, and animals which we consider lower in the evolutionary scale than our beloved dogs have shown that when two intensely inbred lines of consecutive brother and sister matings are crossed, the resultant progeny are larger than the original heterozygous stock and possess hybrid vigor such as the mongrel possesses, which enables him to exist even under environmental neglect.

Can we Collie breeders indulge in such concentrated inbreeding with our stock as has been attempted successfully by scientists with other genetic material? We don't know, simply because it has never been tried. It would be an expensive undertaking to keep two or more lines of direct brother and sister inbreedings in progress; to cull and destroy, always keeping the best pair as breeding partners for the next generation. Lethal faults, hitherto unsuspected in the stock, might become so drastically concentrated that they will bring the experiment to a premature conclusion, even if one had the time, money, and energy to attempt it. But such is the inherent character of germ plasm that one direct outcross will bring complete normality to an inbred line drastically weakened by its own concentrated faults.

It is essential that the breeder have a complete understanding of the merits of inbreeding, for by employing it skillfully, results can be obtained to equal those found in other animal-breeding fields. We must remember that inbreeding in itself creates neither faults nor virtues; it merely strengthens and fixes them in the resulting animals. If the basic stock used is generally good, possessing but few minor faults, then inbreeding will concentrate all those virtues which are so valuable in that basic stock. Inbreeding gives us great breeding worth by its unique ability to produce prepotency and unusual similarity of type. It exposes the "skeletons in the closet" by bringing to light hitherto hidden faults, so that they may be selected against. We do not correct faults by inbreeding; therefore, we merely make them recognizable so they can be eliminated. The end result of inbreeding, coupled with rigid selection, is complete stability of the breeding material.

With certain strains inbreeding can be capricious, revealing organic weaknesses never suspected that result in decreased vitality, abnormalities—physical and mental—or lethal or crippling factors. Unfortunately, it is not possible to foretell results when embarking on such a program, even if seemingly robust and healthy breeding partners are used as a base. The best chance of success generally

Ch. Coverdale's Lady Shan, owned by Mr. T. J. Gardiner. Photo by C. M. Cooke.

comes from the employment of animals which themselves have been strongly inbred and have not been appreciably weakened by it in any way.

An interesting development frequently found in inbreeding is in the extremes produced. The average progeny from inbreeding is equal to the average from line-breeding or outbreeding, but the extremes are greater than those produced by either of the latter breeding methods. Inbreeding, then, is at once capable of producing the best and the worst, and these degrees can be found present in the same litter.

Here again, in inbreeding, as in most of the elements of animal husbandry, we must avoid thinking in terms of human equations. Whether for good or ill, your Collie was man-made, and his destiny and that of his progeny lie in your hands. By selection you improve the strain, culling and killing misfits and monsters. Mankind indulges in no such practice of purification of the race. He mates without any great mental calculation or plan for the future generation.

His choice of a mate is both geographically and socially limited in scope. No one plans this mating of his for the future betterment of the breed. Instead, he is blindly led by emotions labeled "love," and sometimes by lesser romantics, "desire." Perish the thought that we should cast mud upon the scented waters of romance, but for our shepherds we want something vastly better than the hit-and-miss proposition that has generally been the racial procedure of man.

BACKCROSSING

Another type of inbreeding, which is not practiced as much as it should be, is "backcrossing." Here we think largely in terms of the male dog, since the element of time is involved. The process involves finding a superior breeding male who is so magnificent in type that we want to perpetuate his qualities and produce the prototype of this certain individual. This good male is bred to a fine bitch, and the best female pup who is similar to her sire in type is bred back again to her sire. Again, the best female pup is selected and bred

Ch. Westcarrs Whistler, owned by Miss C. Moloney. Photo by C. M. Cooke.

back to her sire. This is continued as long as the male can reproduce, or until weaknesses become apparent (if they do) that make it impractical to continue. If this excellent male seems to have acquired his superiority through the genetic influence of his mother, the first breeding should possibly be the mating of son to mother, and the subsequent breedings as described above. In each litter the bitch retained to backcross to her sire should, of course, greatly mirror the sire's type.

LINE-BREEDING

Line-breeding is a broader kind of inbreeding that conserves valuable characteristics by concentration and gives us some control of type but a lesser control over specific characteristics. It creates "strains" or "families" within the breed which are easily recognized by their similar conformation. This is the breeding method used by

Ch. Mywicks Model Examiner, owned by Mr. J. E. Mycroft. Photo by C. M. Cooke.

most of the larger kennels with varied success, since it is not extreme and therefore relatively safe. It is also the method the neophyte is generally advised to employ for the same reasons.

Specifically, line-breeding entails the selection of breeding partners who have, in their pedigrees, one or more common ancestors. These individuals (or individual) occur repeatedly within the first four or five generations, so that it can be assumed their genetic influence molds the type of succeeding generations. It is a fact that in many breeds success has been obtained by line-breeding to outstanding individuals.

The method varies greatly in intensity, so that some dogs may be strongly line-bred, while others only remotely so. Selection is an important factor here, too, for if we line-breed to procure the specific type of a certain fine animal, then we must select in succeeding generations breeding stock which is the prototype of that individual, or our reason for line-breeding is lost.

One of the chief dangers of line-breeding can be contributed by the breeder of the strain. Many times the breeder reaches a point where he selects his breeding partners on pedigree alone, instead of by individual selection and pedigree combined, within the line.

In some instances intense line-breeding, particularly when the individual line-bred to is known to be prepotent, can have all the strength of direct inbreeding.

To found a strain which has definite characteristics within the breed, the following recommendations can be used as a guide.

1. Decide what few traits are essential and what faults are intolerable. Vigor, fertility, character, and temperament must be included in these essentials.

2. Develop a scoring system and score selected virtues and faults in accordance with your breeding aim. Particular stress should be put upon scoring for individual traits which need improvement.

3. Line-breed consistently to the best individuals produced which, by the progeny test, show that they will further improve the strain. Inbreeding can be indulged in if the animal used is of exceptional quality and with no outstanding faults. Outcrossings can be made to bring in wanted characteristics if they are missing from the basic stock. Relationship need not be close in the foundation animals, since wide outcrosses will give greater variation and therefore offer a much wider selection of desirable trait combinations.

45

Ch. Tideswell Blue Prince, owned by Miss M. K. Gakabelli. Photo by C. M. Cooke.

Every Collie used in this breeding program to establish a strain must be rigidly assessed for individual and breeding excellence and the average excellence of its relative and its progeny.

OUTCROSS BREEDING

Outcross breeding is the choosing of breeding partners whose pedigrees, in the first five or six generations, are free from any common ancestry. With our Collies we cannot outcross in the true sense of the term, since the genetic basis of all Collies, both here and abroad, is based upon the germ plasm of a few selected individuals. To outcross completely, using the term literally (complete heterozygosity), it would be necessary to use an individual of an alien breed as one of the breeding partners.

For the breeder to exercise any control over the progeny of an outcross mating, one of the partners should be inbred or closely line-bred. The other partner should show, in himself and by the progeny test when bred to other bitches, that he is dominant in the needed compensations which are the reasons for the outcross. Thus, by outcross breeding, we bring new and needed characteristics into a strain, along with greater vigor and, generally, a lack of uniformity in the young. Greater uniformity can be achieved if the outcross is made between animals of similar family type. Here again we have a breeding method which has produced excellent individuals, since it tends to conceal recessive genes and promote individual merit, but it generally leads to a lower breeding worth in the outbred animal by dispersing favorable genetic combinations which have given us strain uniformity.

Outcross breeding can be likened to a jigsaw puzzle. We have a puzzle made up of pieces of various shapes and sizes which, when fitted together, form a certain pattern. This basic puzzle is comparable to our line-bred or inbred strain but in this puzzle there are a few pieces that we would like to change, and in so doing change the finished puzzle pattern for the better. We outcross by removing

Ch. Emric Epithet of Dunsinane, owned by Mrs. A. F. Chatfield. Photo by C. M. Cooke.

some of the pieces and reshaping them to our fancy, remembering that these new shapes also affect the shapes of the adjoining pieces which must then be slightly altered for perfect fit. When this has been successfully accomplished, the finished pattern has been altered to suit our pleasure—we hope.

It sometimes happens that a line-bred or inbred bitch will be outcross-bred to a stud possessed of an open pedigree. It would be assumed by the breeder that the bitch's family type would dominate in the resulting progeny. But occasionally the stud proves himself to be strongly prepotent, and the young instead reflect his individual qualities, not those of the bitch. This can be good or bad, depending on what you are looking for in the resultant litter.

Incidentally, when we speak of corrective, or compensation, breeding, we do not mean the breeding of extremes to achieve an intermediate effect. We would not breed an extremely shy bitch to an overaggressive or vicious stud in the hope of getting progeny of good

Ch. Westcarrs Blue Mygirl, owned by Mrs. E. Edgar. Photo by C. M. Cooke.

temperament. The offspring of such a mating would show temperament faults of both the extremes. Neither would we breed a long, level-crouped bitch to a stud whose croup is short and drops off sharply. From such a breeding we could expect either level croups or steep croups, but no intermediate possessing the desired croups. Corrective, or compensation, breeding means the breeding of one partner which is lacking, or faulty, in any specific respect, to an animal which is normal or excellent in the particular area where the other partner is found lacking. In the resulting progeny we can expect to find some young which show the desired improvement.

To sum up briefly, we find that *inbreeding* brings us a fixity of type and simplifies the breeding formula. It strengthens desirable dominants and brings hidden and undesirable recessives to the surface where they can be recognized and possibly corrected by *outcross breeding*. When we have thus established definite improvement in type by rigid selection for wanted characteristics, we *line-breed* to create and establish a strain or family line which, in varying degrees, incorporates and produces the improvements which have been attained.

In this maze of hidden and obvious genetic stirring, we must not forget the importance of the concrete essence that stands before us. The breeding partners must be examined as individuals in themselves, apart from the story their pedigrees tell us, for as individuals they have been fashioned by, and are the custodians of, their germ plasm, and mirror this fact in their being. Breedings made only from paper study are akin to human marriages arranged in youth by a third party without consulting the partners—they can be consummated but have small chance of success.

The importance of a pedigree lies in the knowledge we have of the individual animals involved. A fifteen-generation pedigree means nothing if we know nothing about the dogs mentioned. It is more important to extend your knowledge of three or four generations than to extend the pedigree itself. Of real guidance in breeding is a card-index system. This system should indicate clearly the faults and virtues of every pedigree name for at least three generations, with available information as to dominant and recessive traits and the quality of each animal's progeny. At the moment, such a system is practically impossible to achieve. There is little enough known, genetically, about living animals, and the virtues of dogs that are gone are distorted by time and sentiment. Here is a real project

Ch. Legend of Ladypark, owned by Miss P. M. Grey. Photo by C. M. Cooke.

and a challenge, since true pedigree recordings, correctly developed, can represent a really valuable progeny test of ancestors. To be truly efficacious, near ancestors, as well as litter mates, must also be examined for endowed traits, and percentages with regard to these traits correlated and recorded in the pedigree index. From these indexes, graphs could be plotted which would indicate trends within the breed as a whole. To accomplish this design completely, a geneticist would have to be employed and furnished with absolutely truthful information.

The breeding of fine dogs is not a toy to be played with by children. For some of us it forms a nucleus of living, in the esthetic sense. We who give much of our time, thought, and energy to the production of superior stock are often disgusted and disillusioned by the breeding results of others who merely play at breeding. So often individuals long in the game advise the novice never to inbreed, but only to linebreed, since in this way the least harm can be done. There has been too much harm done already by novice breeders who should not have been encouraged to breed at all, except under the direct supervision or advice of an experienced or knowledgeable dog man.

The people who compose what we term the Collie "fancy," belong to one of three categories: the novice, the amateur, and the professional. The novice is one who has recently become enamored of the breed, a tyro, a beginner. Many of them remain in that category indefinitely, due to lack of sincerity or reluctance to learn. Others, eager to absorb all they can, soon rise above the original status.

The professional is one who makes his livelihood from the dog game. His living or employment depends in whole or part upon his kennel activities. A professional must know his business well in order to make it a success, and the earnest professional generally does, though he may occasionally be guilty of breeding for the market.

Ch. Danvis Damascus, owned by Mr. T. D. Purvis. Photo by C. M. Cooke.

Numerically, the largest category is that of the amateur. To these individuals the breeding, showing, or training of Collies is a serious hobby. Here are the students of the breed, the people who, in most instances, are well informed, yet avid for new knowledge that will aid in breed betterment.

Our novice is many times a charming person who loves his dogs passionately, provides them with more fancy vitamins and supplements than honest food, and treats them with a sloppy sentimentality that even a human baby would resent. He simply can't wait to breed his lovely bitch and have those adorable puppies. Of course he hasn't the time to acquire a bit of knowledge about the breed, or about the animals in his bitch's pedigree or the stud to which he is going to breed. How then will he have the time or knowledge to care for the pregnant bitch and the subsequent litter properly? Yet inevitably he does find time to listen to the pseudo-professional advice of several self-confessed authorities. In due time this novice is possessed

Ch. Conrad's Music Maestro, bred and owned by Roy L. Ayers, Sr.

Undefeated Ch. Braegate Model of Bellhaven.

of from seven to ten of the cutest puppies you ever saw, which will in turn be sold to other novices (Heaven help them) as show and breeding prospects.

What has been written above is not to be construed as a sweeping condemnation of all novices. Without a constant influx of neophyte breeders, the breed would not be in the high place it is today. Many so-called novices bring to their new breed interest a vast store of canine knowledge collected by an inquiring mind and contact with other breeds.

To repeat, the novice is generally advised by the old-time breeder to begin his new hobby with a line-bred bitch, as this is the cautious approach which leaves the least margin for error. But what of that novice who is essentially what we call a born "dog man," that individual who, for lack of better definition, we say has a "feel" for dogs, who seems to possess an added sense where dogs are concerned? If this person has an inquiring mind, normal intelligence, and has been associated with other breeds, then the picture of him as the true novice changes. The old-timer will find many times that this "novice" frequently possesses information that the old-timer did not even know existed. This is especially true if the tyro has been exposed to some scientific learning in fields relative to animal advancement. Even experience, which is the old-timer's last-ditch stand, is negligible, for this knowledgeable "novice" can disregard the vagaries of experience with foreknowledge of expectancy.

In most instances this type of novice doesn't begin to think of breeding, or even owning, a specimen of the breed until he has made a thorough study of background, faults, virtues, and genetic characters. To him, imitation is not a prelude to success. Therefore the line-bred bitch, modeled by another's ego, is not for him. The outcross bitch, whose genetic composition presents a challenge and which, by diligent study and application of acquired knowledge, can become the fountainhead of a strain of his own, is the answer to his need.

Some of what you have read here with reference to the novice may have seemed to be cruel caricature. Actually it is not caricature, but it is cruel and is meant to stress a point. We realize that to some novices our deep absorption in the many aspects of breed betterment may seem silly or ridiculous, but genetic repercussion of breeding stupidity can echo down through generations, making a mockery of our own intense, sometimes heartbreaking and often humble striving toward an ideal.

4.

Coat Color Inheritance in the Collie

Studies of coat color in Collies by geneticists have varied slightly in some details, but the end results arrived at in these studies have been rather uniform in scope. We can be definitely sure that the popular sable color is dominant over tri-color, and that the merle factor is a dominant modifier of the sable and tri-color.

The essential colors of the breed are sable, tri-color, blue merle and white. Sables vary in intensity from dark mahogany to light tan, an almost orange color and a washed out straw color. The intensity desired by the breeder can be arrived at by selection within the color phase. A definite color pattern has been established by selection with regard to the white markings that are so desirable in the breed. The full white collar, white forelegs, feet, tail tip and the extension of the collar white down under the chest is the desirable pattern. Again the amount of white in these areas can be held or changed by selection. This sable color is definitely dominant to non-sable in Collies due to a single gene allelomorphic to the recessive tri-color.

Tri-colored Collies are essentially black dogs with tan markings and white areas. They are recessive to sables and when bred together will produce only tri-colors in their litters. When sables are bred to tri-colors, the resulting young can be either sable or tri-color with the sable-colored puppies far more numerous that the tri-colored offspring, indicating that the sable carries a recessive gene for tri-color.

When two sables are bred they can also produce some tri-colors, but the percentage is quite small in proportion to the number of sable offspring. Again we can assume that the sables used which produce tri-colors carry a recessive for tri-color.

The blue merle color is the result of a dilution factor. It follows the general color pattern of the sables and tri-colored Collies, but the colored areas are broken, allowing white to appear between the colored spots. These merle color areas can be either black or tan or, most frequently, a combination of both affected by the dilution factor. When sable or tri-colored dogs are bred to blue merles, the resultant litters contain all three of these color phases; sable, tri-color and blue merle, in almost equal ratio. Again we can assume from the results that both sables and tri-colors carry the dilution factor in a hidden state.

There are two kinds of whites that can be found in Collies; the dark-eyed whites which exhibit some color on the ears and the root of the tail, and the blue-eyed, which is a "self" white. These two kinds of white dogs are distinctly different genetically. Both are recessive to sable, tri-color and blue merle.

The breeding of top whites is a problem to those who prefer this color (or lack of color) phase. There seems to be a correlation between

Ch. Peterblue Sophie, owned by Miss K. Alexander and Miss E. Dundas Monat.
Photo by C. M. Cooke.

Skyline Diamond Lil, a white bitch with a tri head. Sire: Ch. Shay of Sparton.
Dam: Halocross Nightengale. Owner: Thelma Brown.

white and lack of the distinctive type arrived at in the more colorful Collies. It was found that by breeding blue merle to blue merle an even greater degree of dilution occurred and eventually the animals obtained from this practice could be rated as whites. But the "wall" or "China eye" became more marked and we know that defective sight and deafness are associated with homozygous merle dilution in Collies.

To keep type and coat quality the better practice is to cross the best whites to the finest sables or tri-colors, select from the offspring those that display the most of the wanted virtues and breed them back again to the best whites. By selection your whites can thus be upgraded. But, if there is a limiting factor involved, and there seems to be, it will be the rare white who can approach the quality of the colored Collies. Incidentally, the blue-eyed white, when bred to a tri-color, can produce the merle color and, by mating two merles together, the undesirable blue-eyed white can be produced.

The following chart might help to clarify coat color inheritance.

COLORS PAIRED	OFFSPRING COLOR EXPECTANCY
sable × sable	sable and tri-color with sable greatly predominating.
sable × tri-color	sable and tri-color with more sable than tri but less than sable × sable
sable × merle	sable, tri-color and merle in equal ratio
tri-color × merle	sable, tri-color and merle
tri-color × tri-color	all tri-color
sable × white	sable, tri-color (few), merle (few), white (large percentage)
merle × merle	merle
merle × white	merle, white
white × white	white (large percentage), merle
white × spotted	sable, spotted whites (large percentage)
spotted × spotted	spotted whites

Another interesting color note was reported by Dr. Alan L. Mitchell, who studied Collie coat color inheritance and reported his findings in the Journal of Heredity. Dr. Mitchell claims that so-called tri-color is a bicolor, not a tan modified, and he shows that the blue merle is a modification of the bicolor due to a dominant factor, so that the blue merle color cannot appear unless it is accompanied by the tri-color pattern also.

In summing up the coat color inheritance in Collies we find that sable is dominant over tri-color, but that very few sables are pure for their color and carry recessives. Blue merle is the product of a dilution factor and is a dominant modifier of the sable and the tri-color and that the pairing of blue merles can result in a proportion of blue-eyed whites. Tri-colors, when bred together, can produce nothing but tri-colors, but two sables can throw tri-colors in their litters, showing that the solid color in Collies is incompletely dominant to black and tan but is a simple dominant to the white color. Deafness and defective sight is associated with merle dilution in the homozygous condition in Collies.

In any of the various color phases the Collie is a striking and majestic dog. The color you select is a matter of privileged taste and whatever the color you choose, you can be sure that you have selected one of the finest breeds of dogs.

5.

Feeding

Your dog is a carnivore, a flesh eater. His teeth are not made for grinding as are human teeth, but are chiefly fashioned for tearing and severing. Over a period of years this fact has led to the erroneous conclusion that the dog must be fed mostly on muscle meat in order to prosper. Wolves, jackals, wild dogs, and foxes comprise the family Canidae to which your dog belongs. These wild relatives of the dog stalk and run down their living food in the same manner the dog would employ if he had not become attached to man. The main prey of these predators are the various hoofed herbivorous animals, small mammals and birds of their native habitat. The carnivores consume the entire body of their prey, not just the muscle meat alone. This manner of feeding has led some zoologists to consider the dog family as omnivorous (eater of both plant and animal matter), despite their obvious physical relationship to the carnivores.

You would assume, and rightly so, that the diet which keeps these wild cousins of the dog strong, healthy, and fertile could be depended upon to do the same for your Collie. Of course, in this day and age your dog cannot live off the land. He depends upon you for sustenance, and to feed him properly you must understand what essential food values the wild carnivore derives from his kill, for this is nature's supreme lesson in nutrition.

The canine hunter first laps the blood of his victim, then tears open the stomach and eats its contents, composed of predigested vegetable matter. He feasts on liver, heart, kidneys, lungs, and the fat-encrusted intestines. He crushes and consumes the bones and the marrow they contain, feeds on fatty meat and connective tissue, and finally eats the lean muscle meat. From the blood, bones, marrow, internal organs, and muscle meat he has absorbed minerals and proteins. The stomach and its contents have supplied vitamins and carbohydrates. From the intestines and fatty meat he gets fats, fatty acids, vitamins, and carbohydrates. Other proteins come from the ligaments and connective tissue. Hair and some indigestible parts of the intestinal contents provide enough roughage for proper laxation. From the sun he basks in and the water he drinks, he absorbs supplementary vitamins and minerals. From his kill, therefore, the carnivore acquires a well-rounded diet. To supply these same essentials to your Collie in a form which you can easily purchase is the answer to his dietary needs.

BASIC FOODS AND SUPPLEMENTS

From the standpoint of nutrition, any substance may be considered food which can be used by an animal as a body-building material, a source of energy, or a regulator of body activity. From the preceding paragraphs we have learned that muscle meat alone will not fill these needs and that your Collie's diet must be composed of many other food materials to provide elements necessary to his growth and health. These necessary ingredients can be found in any grocery store. There you can buy all the important natural sources of the dietary essentials listed below.

1. PROTEIN: meat, dairy products, eggs, soybeans.
2. FAT: butter, cream, oils, fatty meat, milk, cream cheese, suet.
3. CARBOHYDRATES: cereals, vegetables, confectionery, syrups, honey.
4. VITAMIN A: greens, peas, beans, asparagus, broccoli, eggs, milk.
5. THIAMINE: vegetables, legumes, whole grains, eggs, muscle meats, organ meats, milk, yeast.
6. RIBOFLAVIN: green leaves, milk, *liver*, cottonseed flour or meal, egg yolk, wheat germ, yeast, beef, chicken.
7. NIACIN: milk, lean meats, liver, yeast.
8. VITAMIN D: fish that contains oil (salmon, sardine, herring, cod), fish liver oils, eggs, fortified milk.
9. ASCORBIC ACID: tomatoes, citrus fruits, raw cabbage (it has not been established that ascorbic acid is necessary for dogs).
10. IRON, CALCIUM, AND PHOSPHORUS: milk and milk products, vegetables, eggs, soybeans, bone marrow, blood, liver, oatmeal.

The first three listed essentials complement each other and compose the basic nutritional needs. Proteins build new body tissue and are composed of amino acids, which differ in combination with the different proteins. Carbohydrates furnish the fuel for growth and energy, and fat produces heat which becomes energy and enables the dog to store energy against emergency. Vitamins and minerals, in general, act as regulators of cell activity.

Proteins are essentially the basis of life, for living cells are composed of protein molecules. In this connection, an interesting

Though it is theoretically possible for you to make a Collie food with all of the essential elements in it, it is much cheaper to buy it in the form of dry or canned dog food already manufactured for the purpose. Dog foods are more closely regulated by the Federal Government than human foods. Photo by Louise Van der Meid.

scientific experiment was conducted a short while ago which led to an important discovery. A young scientist attempted to duplicate the conditions which, it is assumed, prevailed upon the earth before life began. Cosmological theory indicates that the atmosphere at that time (approximately two thousand million years ago, give or take a year) would have been poisonous to all the living organisms that exist today, with the exception of certain bacteria. When the experiment had been completed, it was found that amino acids had formed.

Ch. Bellhaven's Blue Lucason.

These chemicals are the building blocks of proteins, and proteins are the basis of life. No, science has not yet produced actual life by building proteins. It is still rather difficult to even define life, let alone manufacture it. But we can sustain and give growth to living forms by proper feeding procedures.

The main objective in combining food factors is to mix them in the various amounts necessary to procure a balanced diet. This can be done in a number of ways. The essential difference in the many good methods of feeding lies in the time it takes to prepare the food and in the end cost of the materials used. Dogs can be fed expensively and they can be fed cheaply, and in each instance they can be fed equally well.

There are various food products on the market packaged specifically for canine consumption. The quality of these foods as complete diets in themselves ranges from poor to excellent. The better *canned*, or *pudding*, foods are good but expensive for large breeds such as ours, since the moisture content is high and your Collie must consume a large amount for adequate nourishment. Compact and requiring no preparation, the canned foods are fine for use at shows or when traveling—though for traveling an even better diet is biscuits, lean meat, and very little water. The result is less urination and defecation, since the residue from this diet is very small. The diet is, of course, not to be fed over any extended period of time because it lacks food-value.

Biscuits can be considered as tidbits rather than food, since much of the vitamin and mineral content has been destroyed by baking. The same holds true for *kibbled* foods. They are fillers to which must be added fat, milk, broths, meat, vegetables, and vitamin and mineral supplement.

By far the most complete of the manufactured foods are the *grain foods*. In such a highly competitive business as the manufacturing and merchandising of these foods, it is essential for the manufacturer to market a highly palatable and balanced ration. The better grain foods have constantly changing formulas to conform to the most recent results of scientific dietary research. They are, in many cases,

Canadian and American Ch. Windswept Domino Jac. Photo by Wm. Brown.

Dry dog foods are excellent for Collies because they are such heavy feeders. When you add the water, it is a good idea to add some vitamin and mineral supplements as well.

the direct result of controlled generation tests in scientific kennels where their efficacy can be ascertained. A good grain food should not be considered merely a filler. Rather, it should be employed as the basic diet to which fillers might possibly be added. Since the grain food is bag or box packaged and not hermetically sealed, the fat content is necessarily low. A high degree of fat would produce quick rancidity. Therefore fat must be added to the dry food. Milk, which is one of the finest of foods in itself, can be added along with broth or plain warm water to arrive at the proper consistency for palatability. With such a diet we have a true balance of essentials, wastage is kept to a minimum, stools are small and firm and easily removed, and cost and labor have been reduced to the smallest equation possible to arrive at and yet feed well. The *pellet-type* food is simply grain food to which a binding agent has been added to hold the grains together in the desired compact form.

Fat should be introduced into the dog's diet in its pure form. Proteins and carbohydrates are converted into fat by the body. Fat also causes the dog to retain his food longer in the stomach. It stores vitamins E, K, A, and D, and lessens the bulk necessary to be fed at each meal. Fat can be melted and poured over the meal, or put through the meat grinder and then mixed with the basic ration.

Just as selection is important in breeding, so ratio is important in feeding. The proper diet must not only provide all the essentials, it must also supply those essentials in proper proportion. This is what we mean by a balanced diet. It can be dangerous to your Collie's well being if the ratios of any of his dietary essentials are badly unbalanced over a period of time. The effect can be disastrous in the case of puppies. This is the basic reason for putting your faith in a good, scientifically balanced grain dog food.

There is an abundance of concentrated *vitamin supplements* on the market specifically manufactured for dogs. They are undoubtedly

Water should always be available to Collies. Dogs which are kept outdoors should always have fresh, clean water available. There are many devices available which can be attached to your garden hose which lets the Collie have the water as he needs it. Photo by Louise Van der Meid.

of real worth—if your dog needs a supplement. Dogs fed a balanced diet do not need additional concentrated supplements. If you feel that your dog is in need of a supplement, it is wiser to consult your veterinarian for advice and specific dosage. Check the label of the dog food you buy to make sure that it has all the necessary ingredients. If it has, you will not find it necessary to pour in concentrated, highly expensive supplements. A supplement widely in use today, packaged under various trade names, embodies the elements of what was initially called A.P.F., or animal protein factor. This is a powder combining various antibiotic residues with the composite vitamin B_{12}. The role of this supplement in dog feeding has not, as yet, been adequately established. Theoretically, it is supposed that this supplement produces better food utilization and the production of extra body fat, which accounts for better growth and weight. On the other hand, it is also thought that it can affect the normal balance of intestinal flora, and overdoses can produce undesirable effects. Nature is generally generous in her gift of vitamins, minerals, and

This is a commercial Collie Kennel. It is only in such establishments that it pays to mix your own foods. The individual Collie owner should be satisfied to buy dog food already prepared, either in the can or dry, in a bag.

other nutritional essentials, and all can be found, in adequate abundance, in the balanced diet. We do not want to rule out supplements, but we do want to stress that they should be used with care.

In many instances kennel owners feel that their animals, for various reasons, need a supplementary boost in their diet. Some are in critical stages of growth, bitches are about to be bred or are in whelp, mature dogs are being frequently used for stud, and others are recuperating from illness. In such cases supplements can be added to the food, but in reasonable amounts. It is better, too, to supply the supplements through the medium of natural nutritional material, rather than chemical, concentrated, commercial supplements. Brewers' yeast, alfalfa meal, and similar natural agents can be mixed separately in a container and judicious quantities added to the basic diet.

Calcium and *phosphorus* in pure chemical form must be handled with care when used in the dog's diet. Toxic conditions can be caused by an overabundance of this material in the bloodstream. Green, ground, edible bone meal is a much better product to use where it is thought necessary. Most good grain foods have an abundance of this inexpensive element in correct balance. Milk is a highly desirable vehicle for balanced calcium and phosphorus as well as many other nutritional needs.

Cod liver oil is another product that, if given to excess over a period of time, can cause toxicity and bone malformation. It is better and cheaper to employ a fish liver oil concentrate such as percomorph oil. In this oil the base vehicle has been discarded and the pure oil concentrated, so that a very small dosage is required. Many owners and breeders pour cod liver oil and throw handfuls of calcium and supplementary concentrates into the food pans in such lavish amounts that there is a greater bulk of these than of the basic food, on the theory that, if a little does some good, a greater amount will be of immense benefit. This concept is both ridiculous and dangerous.

An occasional pinch of *bicarbonate of soda* in the food helps to neutralize stomach acidity and can prevent, or alleviate, fatigue caused by a highly acid diet. Bones need never be fed to dogs for food value if the diet is complete. Poultry bones should never be fed. They splinter into sharp shards which can injure gums or rip the throat lining or intestines. Once in the stomach they are dissolved by strong gastric juices. It is on their way to their ultimate goal that they do damage. The same is also true of fishbones. Soft rib bones are excellent to feed your dog periodically, not necessarily as nourishment, but to clean his teeth. The animal's teeth pierce through them completely, and in so doing tartar is removed and the teeth are kept clean of residue. These soft rib bones can be considered the canine's toothbrush.

Table scraps are always good, and if your dog is a good eater and easy keeper, give him any leftovers in his food pan, including potatoes. The diets of good feeders can be varied to a greater extent without unfavorable repercussions than can the diets of finicky eaters. Fish is a good food, containing all the food elements which are found in meat, with a bonus of extra nutritional values. *Muscle meat* lacks

Ch. Pattingham Gay Lady of Glenmist, owned by Mrs. M. R. Franklin.
Photo by C. M. Cooke.

Ch. Hughley Blue Rocket, owned by Mrs. M. S. Rhys. Photo by C. M. Cooke.

many essentials and is so low in calcium that even when supplemented with vitamin D, there is grave danger of rickets developing. In its raw state, meat is frequently the intermediate host of several forms of internal parasites. Meat by-products and canned meat, which generally contains by-products, are much better as food for dogs than pure muscle meat. Incidentally, whale meat, which is over 80 per cent protein, could well replace horse meat, which is less than 50 per cent protein, in the dog's diet.

Water is one of the elementary nutritional essentials. Considering the fact that the dog's body is approximately 70 per cent water, which is distributed in varying percentages throughout the body tissues and organs, including the teeth and bones, it isn't difficult to realise the importance of this staple to the dog's well being. Water flushes the system, stimulates gastric juice activity, brings about better appetite, and acts as a solvent within the body. It is one of the major sources of necessary minerals and helps during hot weather, and to a

Ch. Beulah's Blanco-y-Negro, owned by Mrs. N K. George. Photo by C. M. Cooke.

lesser degree during winter, to regulate the dog's temperature. When a dog is kept from water for any appreciable length of time dehydration occurs. This is a serious condition, a fact which is known to any dog owner whose animal has been affected by diarrhea, continuous nausea, or any of the diseases in which this form of body shrinkage occurs.

Water is the cheapest part of your dog's diet, so supply it freely, particularly in warm weather. In winter if snow and ice are present and available to your Collie, water is not so essential. At any rate, if left in a bucket in his run, it quickly turns to ice. Yet even under these conditions it is an easy matter to bring your dog in and supply him with at least one good drink of fresh water during the day. Being so easily provided, so inexpensive, and so highly essential to your Collie's health, sober thought dictates that we should allow our dogs to "take to drink."

Breeders with only a few dogs can sometimes afford the extra time, expense, and care necessary to feed a varied and complicated diet, but it is easy to see that to feed a large kennel in such fashion would take an immense amount of time, labor, and expense. Actually, the feeding of a scientifically balanced grain food as the basic diet eliminates the element of chance which exists in diets prepared by the kennel owner from natural sources, since overabundance of some specific elements, as well as a lack of others, can bring about dietary ills and deficiencies.

Caloric requirements vary with age, temperament, changes in temperature, and activity. If your dog is nervous, very active, young, and kept out of doors in winter, his caloric intake must be greater than the phlegmatic, underactive, fully grown dog who has his bed in the house. Keep your Collie in good flesh, neither too fat nor too thin. You are best judge of the amount to feed him to keep him in his best condition. A well-fed Collie should always be in show "bloom"— clear-eyed, glossy-coated, filled with vim and vigor, and with enough of an all-over layer of fat to give him sleekness without plumpness.

Water is the cheapest part of your Collie's diet, so supply it constantly. A Collie can live much longer without food than without water.

FEEDING TECHNIQUES

The consistency of the food mix can vary according to your dog's taste. It is best not to serve the food in too sloppy a mixture, except in the case of very young puppies. It is also good practice to feed the same basic ration at every meal so that the taste of the food does not vary greatly at each feeding. Constant changing of the diet, with supplementary meals of raw or cooked meat, tends to produce finicky eaters, the bane of the kennel and private owner's existence. Never leave the food pan before your dog for more than thirty minutes. If he hasn't eaten by then, or has merely nibbled, the pan should be removed and not presented to him again until his next feeding time. This same policy should be followed when breaking a dog to a new diet. If he has become a canine gourmet, spoiled by a delicate diet, he may sometimes refuse to eat for two or three days but eventually, when his hunger becomes acute enough and he realizes his hunger strike will not result in coddling and the bringing forth of his former delicacies, he will eat with gusto whatever is put before him. Remember, your Collie is not a lap dog—he is a big and powerful working dog and should not be babied. Where there are several dogs to create mealtime competition, there is little danger of finicky eaters regardless of what is fed.

Keep your feeding utensils clean to eliminate the danger of bacterial formation and sourness, especially in warm weather. Your food pans can be of any solid metal material. Agate, porcelain, and the various type of enamelware have a tendency to chip and are therefore not desirable.

Every kennel owner and breeder has his own pet diet which has proven successful in the rearing and maintenance of his stock. In each instance he will insist that his is the only worth-while diet and he cannot be blamed for so asserting, since his particular diet has nourished and kept his own stock in top condition over a period of years. Yet the truth is, as we have mentioned before in this chapter, that there are many ways to feed dogs and feed them well and no one diet can be said to be the best.

Perhaps it would be enlightening to the reader to explain how the dogs are fed in the kennels of three different breeders. The results of these three different diets have all been excellent. There have been no runts; the growth factor in each instance has been entirely adequate and none of the animals bred or raised have shown any signs of nutritional lack. All the dogs raised on these diets have developed normally into the full flower of their genetic inheritance with lustrous coats, fine teeth and bones, and all possessing great vigor and stamina. Incidentally, what has been written in this chapter is applicable mostly to grown dogs, though the three feeding formulas to follow include puppy feeding as well. A more comprehensive study of puppy feeding will be found in the chapter dealing specifically with puppies.

Diet Number 1

Dietol, an oil product, is given the pups in the nest on the second day after whelping; two drops to each puppy. The amount is gradually increased until the second week each pup is receiving ten drops of the oil. The third week twenty drops are given and this is continued until a full pint has been consumed.

At twelve to fourteen days, for a litter of six puppies, a cereal is cooked with one-eighth of a pound of butter or margarine or a good special puppy meal is substituted for the cereal. To this is added one-half a can of evaporated milk, two poached eggs, cow's milk, and two tablespoonfuls of Karo syrup. This is fed twice daily to supplement dam's feedings.

The amount of food that a Collie requires varies with his age, size, temperament, activity and the temperature in which the dog lives. Collies maintained outdoors are in more need of food than Collies kept indoors.

Well fed Collie puppies have a well fed look. You don't have to be an expert to see that these Collie pups have been well cared for.

At three weeks the same diet is given three times a day.

At four weeks the same diet is given four times a day. At this time chopped beef, rich in fat, is added, and two eggs are cooked in with the cereal.

Between the fifth and sixth weeks the puppies are weaned. During this period two feedings are the same as the diet fed during the fourth week, and two other feedings are composed of a good grain dog meal, moistened with broth or soup, to which has been added a heaping handful of chopped beef which is at least 25 per cent fat. This food mixture is supplemented by three tablespoons of refined cod liver oil and a heaping tablespoon of a mixture of bone meal, soybean meal, brewer's yeast, and a small amount of salt.

Three meals are fed as described above at three months and continued until the pups have reached the age of five months, the only variation being the use of small kibbles occasionally replacing the basic cereal or meal at two of the meals.

From five months until twelve to fourteen months two large meals are given, one in the morning and one at night, using the same diet as above, augmented by any and all table scraps, from potatoes and sauerkraut to cake.

From fourteen months on the dog is fed once daily in the summer. In fall and winter the diet consists of a light breakfast of warm cereal, milk, and Karo syrup. The main evening meal is composed of grain meal, or occasionally, kibbles or pellets, moistened in soup or warm water, a pound of ground fatty meat, one tablespoonful of cod liver oil or Dietol, and a heaping tablespoon of the mixed supplement mentioned previously (bone meal, soybean meal, and yeast). To this is added table scraps of every description, except fowl bones and fishbones.

During the winter months occasional stews of beef or lamb and fresh vegetables are cooked and relished by the Collies.

Diet Number 2

Dietol is given each puppy in increasing amounts as it grows, beginning with two drops for Collie puppies. This oil is rich in vitamin K, which is an essential vitamin for puppy survival.

At sixteen days the pups are given their first supplementary feeding. From then on the Dietol is incorporated in their meals. A puppy grain meal, Pampa, is used as a base, to which is added a tablespoonful of Pelargon, a Nestle's dried milk product which has been enriched and acidified so that it more closely approaches the taste of the bitch's milk than does plain cow's milk. (Incidentally, if you've brought a puppy home who refuses to eat, try this product mixed with warm milk or sprinkled over the food mixture. In almost every instance it will do the trick.) Warmed cow's milk and about 10 per cent melted fat is added to the Pampa and Pelargon. Stir to the consistency of cream and allow them to eat all they can hold.

At three weeks the same mixture is fed three times a day.

At four weeks, the same mixture is fed four times a day. The fat content is raised to about 15 per cent. The consistency of the food is slightly thickened, and a natural supplement, composed of alfalfa leaf meal, irradiated yeast, and ground bone meal, is added sparingly. The ratios of these ingredients, mixed together in a large jar for continued use are: two tablespoonfuls of alfalfa leaf meal to one tablespoonful of yeast and three-quarters of a tablespoonful of bone meal.

At six weeks the pups are completely weaned and fed five times daily. Four of the meals are the same mixture as used at four weeks, with a small amount of canned horse meat added for taste and a scent appeal. The meals are increased in size with the growth of the pups. The last meal, the fifth at night, consists of warmed milk, half natural cow and half evaporated. After eight weeks the Pelargon is discontinued and powdered milk is used instead.

Five feedings are given until three months; four feedings from then up to five months.

From five months until eight months three feedings are given, eliminating the late evening milk meal. The dog is switched then from Pampa to a regular grain meal (in this instance either Lifespan or Kasco, since both are easily available and are good grain foods). Milk is added to all other meals in powder or liquid form.

Two meals from eight to eighteen months are fed and thereafter one meal, unless, as is generally the case, the individual thrives better on two meals.

Table scraps of all kinds are used whenever available, exclusive of fowl bones and fishbones. The schedule as outlined above is not

If you have a large number of Collie pups to feed, and money is a problem, you can change the milk part of the diet to water after the pups are three to four months old.

necessarily a rigid one. Fish, stews, eggs (yokes only if raw, whole egg if cooked), liver, and a host of other foods are occasionally incorporated into the diet, but this is the one main day in, day out diet.

Diet Number 3

This diet is used by a breeder of Redbone coon hounds. During the hunting season they are hunted extensively, running miles and miles of woodland nightly, trailing their quarry. Bitches are bred regularly, whelping large litters of healthy pups.

At sixteen to eighteen days supplementary feeding is begun, consisting of Pampa (or a like product) and warmed evaporated milk. This mixture (of creamy consistency) is fed three times a day.

At seven weeks the puppies are completely weaned and receive four feedings daily as described above. Fat is now added to the diet to the amount of 20 per cent of the dry weight of the complete ration.

This amount of fat is incorporated into the diet until the puppies are three to four months of age. At this time the pups are changed to a tested adult grain meal and the fat incorporated raised to 25 per cent of the dry total. The pups are then fed twice daily with hot water replacing the milk, until fully grown.

With full growth only one daily feeding is given, consisting of the same diet as above.

To the earnest breeder, working with a limited amount of stock, every breeding made is the result of intense study and much discussion, since every breeding made is eminently important and must not be wasted. Then, to complement the results of breeding, a complete and balanced diet is necessary to follow through and bring the resulting get to a correct and healthy maturity.

Remember always that feeding ranks next to breeding in the influence it exerts on the growing dog. Knowledgeable breeding can produce genetically fine specimens, selection can improve the strain and the breed, but, without full and proper nourishment, particularly over the period of growth, the dog cannot attain to the promise of his heritage. The brusque slogan of a famous cattle breeder might well be adopted by breeders of Collies. The motto is, "Breed, feed, weed."

6.
General Care

When you own a dog you own a dependent. Though the Internal Revenue Department does not recognize this fact, it is nevertheless true. Whatever pleasure one gets out of life must be paid for in some kind of coin, and this is as applicable to the pleasure we derive from our dogs as it is in all other things. With our dogs we pay the toll of constant care. This dog which you have taken into your home and made a part of your family life depends completely upon you for his every need. In return for the care you give him, he repays you with a special brand of love and devotion that can't be duplicated. This is the bargain you make with your dog: your care on one side of the scale, his complete idolatry on the other. Not quite a fair bargain, but we humans, unlike our dogs, are seldom completely fair and unselfish.

Good husbandry pays off in dollars and cents too, particularly if you have more than one or two dogs, or run a semicommercial kennel. Clean, well-cared-for dogs are most often healthy dogs, free from parasitic invaders and the small ills that bring other and greater woes in their wake. Good feeding and proper exercise help build strength and resistance to disease and a sizable run keeps your canine friend from wandering into the path of some speeding car. Veterinarian bills and nursing time are substantially reduced when your dog is properly cared for, thus saving you money and time.

Cleanliness, that partner to labor which is owned by some to be next to godliness, is the first essential of good dog care. This applies to the dog's surrounding environment as well as to the dog himself. If your Collie sleeps in the house, provide him with a draft-free spot for his bed, away from general household traffic. This bed can be a piece of rug or a well-padded dog mattress. It doesn't particularly matter what material is used as long as it is kept clean and put in the proper place.

Feeding has been comprehensively discussed in the previous chapter, but the utensils used and the methods of feeding come more specifically under the heading of general care, so we will repeat these few facts mentioned in the previous chapter. Heavy aluminum feeding pans are best, since they are easily cleaned and do not chip as do agate or porcelain. Feed your dog regularly in the same place and at the same time. Establish a friendly and quiet atmosphere during feeding periods and do not coax him to eat. If he refuses the food or nibbles at it sparingly, remove his food and do not feed again until the next feeding period. Never allow a pan of food to stand before a healthy dog for more than thirty minutes under any circumstances. Should your dog's appetite continue to be off, consult your veterinarian for the cause.

If you are feeding several dogs in an outside kennel, it is good practice to remain until all are finished, observing their appetites and eating habits while you wait. Often two dogs, kenneled together and given the same amount and kind of food, show different results. One will appear thin and the other in good condition. Sometimes

A lovely little lady with her white Collie. Children can have fun with Collies, but at feeding time train the children to allow their pet Collie to eat without being disturbed.

Count 'em! There are twelve Collie pups and they all came from one Collie bitch. Be careful that every puppy has enough to eat. Check the pups after each meal and be sure that every one has had his ration. Sometimes a shy puppy will actually starve because it cannot compete for the food.

the reason is a physiological one, but more often observation will show that the thinner dog is a slower eater than his kennel mate; that the latter dog gulps down his own food and then drives the thin dog away from his food pan before his ration is fully consumed and finishes this extra portion, too.

Never, never, force-feed a healthy dog simply because he refuses an occasional meal. Force-feeding and coaxing make finicky eaters and a finicky feeder is never in good coat or condition and turns feeding time into the most exasperating experience of the day. Rather than forcing or coaxing, it is better to starve your dog, showing no sympathy at all when he refuses food. If he is healthy, he will soon realize that he will experience hunger unless he eats when the food pan is put before him and will soon develop a normal and healthy appetite. Immediately upon removing the food pans, they should be thoroughly washed and stacked, ready for the next mealtime.

During hot weather, be certain that your dog has a constant supply of fresh, clean water. In winter, water left outside in runs will freeze solid and be of no use to the dog, so it is best to provide fresh water two or three times a day and remove the pail after the dog has had his fill. Always provide water within an hour after feeding.

It has been the experience of most dog people that animals kept or kenneled outdoors, both winter and summer, are healthier and in better condition generally than their softer living housedog brethren. Light and the seasons have a great deal to do with shedding and coat condition. The outdoor dog, living in an environment approaching the natural, has regular shedding periods, after which his new coat comes in hard, strong, and glossy. Housedogs living in conditions of artificial light and heat seem to shed constantly and seldom possess the good coat exhibited by the Collie who lives outdoors. The housedog is much more susceptible to quick changes in temperature, particularly in the winter when he is brought from a warm furnace-heated house into the frigid out-of-doors. Never forget that your dog is a working dog, not a lap dog, and treat him accordingly. Babying an individual of a breed of such high intelligence can produce a nuisance or a canine hypochondriac.

PLANNING YOUR RUN

Even the housedog should be provided with an outside run and house, a domain of his own to keep him in the sun and air and protect him from disturbance by children or other dogs. There, in his run, he is safe from accident, and you know he can't run away to become lost, strayed, or stolen. There, also, you can be sure he is not soiling or digging in your neighbor's newly planted lawn, a situation which can strain, to put it mildly, any "good-neighbor policy." Provide shade in some section of the run against the hot summer sun. Natural shade from trees is the ideal, of course, but artificial shade can be provided by a strategically placed canvas overthrow.

The run should be as large as your property will permit. Twenty by forty feet is a good size for one or two dogs, but if space permits, a longer run is preferable. If you are building a kennel of several runs, remember that the length is more important than the width, and connecting runs in a row can be cut down to ten feet or less in width if the length provided is ample.

The best surface for your run is a question open for argument. Some breeders prefer packed-down fine cinders for their run surface, claiming that this material provides good drainage and is the best surface for a dog's feet, keeping them compact and strong. Actually, heredity and to a lesser degree, diet, are the prime factors that produce good feet in dogs, but a dog's feet will spread and lose compactness if he is kept constantly on a soft or muddy surface. Cinders do make an excellent run, but this surface also makes an admirable place in which parasitic eggs and larvae can exist and thrive, and they are almost impossible to clean out from such a surface, short of resorting to a blowtorch. Many kennel owners favor concrete runs. They are easy to clean and present a good appearance. But again, we have a porous surface in which the minute eggs of parasites can take refuge. Only by daily scrubbing with a strong disinfectant, or periodic surface burning, can concrete runs be kept free of parasitic eggs and larvae.

Gravel and plain dirt runs present the same disadvantage plus the difficulty of efficiently gathering stools from such surfaces. Dirt runs also become muddy in rainy weather and dusty in dry weather, making it necessary to change bedding often, thus producing a deleterious effect upon the animal's feet. It would seem, then, that none of these run surfaces is the perfect answer to our problem. But there is yet another run surface which can give us better control over parasitic reinfestation. On this run we employ washed builders' sand for the surface. The dog generally defecates in a limited area, almost always at the end of his run farthest from the run door and his own house. Stools can easily be removed from the sand surface, and by digging down and removing one or two inches of sand below the stool, parasitic invaders are also removed. Fresh sand is filled into the spaces left by cleaning. The sand soon packs down and becomes a solid surface. The grains drop easily from the dog's feet and are not carried into his house to soil his bedding. This sand is not expensive and the whole surface can be removed periodically and fresh sand brought in and leveled. An ideal run would be one with a cement base which can be washed down with disinfectants or a strong borax solution (which will destroy hookworm larvae) whenever the surface sand is completely removed and before a fresh sand surface is provided.

Not all Collies can be champions . . . and not all Collies are meant to be. Whether your Collie is a champion or not, he should have a name tag in case he strays or gets lost.

Your run should have a lock on the gate so that mischievous children won't open the gate to allow your dogs to roam. Terrible misbreedings can happen this way.

BUILDING YOUR RUN

If you plan to build the run yourself, you might consider the "soil-cement" surface as a base rather than true cement. Soil-cement is a subsurface employed on light-traffic airfields and many suburban roads; it is inexpensive, durable, and easily built without special knowledge or equipment. First remove the sod on the area to be converted into a run, then loosen the soil to a depth of about

84

four inches with a spade and pulverize the soil, breaking up any lumps with a rake. Scatter dry cement at the rate of two-thirds of a sack of cement to a square yard of surface and mix in thoroughly with the soil until the mixture has a floury texture. Adjust your hose to a mist spray and water the surface until the soil-cement mixture will mold under pressure and not crumble. Follow by raking the entire mixture to full depth to assure uniform moisture and level at the same time. Now you must work quickly, compacting the run with a tamper and then rolling with a garden roller. All this must be done within a half hour or the surface will harden while still uneven. After rolling, the surface should be smooth and even. Mist-spray again, then cover with a coating of damp sawdust or soil for a week, after which the run can be used. Remember to keep a slight slope on all run surfaces so that water can drain off without puddling. Soil-cement is also excellent for paths around, or to and from, the kennels.

CLEANING YOUR RUN

In removing stools from a run, never rake them together first. This practice tends to spread worm eggs over a greater area. Shovel each stool up separately and deposit it in a container. When the run is clean, carry the container to a previously prepared pit, dump the contents, and cover with a layer of dirt. Hose out the container and apply disinfectant, and the job is done with a minimum of bother. In winter, due to snow and ice, very little can be done about run sanitation. But those who live in climates which have definite and varied seasons have the consolation of knowing that worm eggs do not incubate nor fleas develop during cold weather. Therefore they must only do whatever is possible in run cleanliness for the sake of appearance and to keep down odors.

FENCING YOUR RUN

Fencing the run is our next problem. The ideal fencing is heavy chain link with metal supporting posts set in cement erected by experts. If your pocketbook cries at such an expenditure (and the cost is not small), you can do your own fencing, cutting the cost drastically by purchasing cheaper wire, using cedar posts for supports, and girding your loins for a bit of labor. Hog wire, six-inch stay wire fencing, fox wire, or fourteen gauge, or two-inch-mesh poultry wire all can be used. Whatever fencing you employ, be sure it is high enough to rise six feet above ground level and is of a heavy enough gauge to be substantial. A mature dog can easily scale fencing which is less than six feet high. Dig post holes, using horizontally stretched string as a guide to keep them evenly in line, and dig them deeply enough to hold the posts securely. Leave approximately six feet of space between each post hole. Paint with creosote, or some other good wood preservative, the sections of the posts which are to be buried in the holes and set the posts in the holes. Concrete and rock, poured into the hole around the post, will provide a firm base. A horizontal top rail strengthens the run materially and will make for a better job. Brace all corner and gate posts as shown in the illustration. When your posts are in and set, borrow a wire stretcher for use in applying the wire fencing to the posts. This handy instrument can make the difference between a poor and a good job.

YOUR DOG HOUSE

The dog house can be simple or elaborate, reaching the extremes from a barrel set on cement blocks to a miniature human dwelling complete with shingles and windows. The best kind of house comes somewhere in between these two extremes. Build the house large enough, with sleeping quarters approximately 3 by 5 feet and 3 feet high at the highest point. Incorporate a front porch $1\frac{1}{2}$ to 2 feet deep and the 5-foot width of the house. If the house is correctly situated, the porch roof offers shade from the sun and the porch itself a place to lie in rainy ro snowy weather. Make the skeleton framework of two by threes, first building the two side sections, allowing six inches of extra height on the uprights for floor elevation. Incorporate the porch size in the over-all length of the side pieces and remember

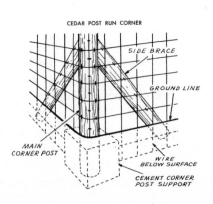

CEDAR POST RUN CORNER

SIDE BRACE

GROUND LINE

MAIN CORNER POST

WIRE BELOW SURFACE

CEMENT CORNER POST SUPPORT

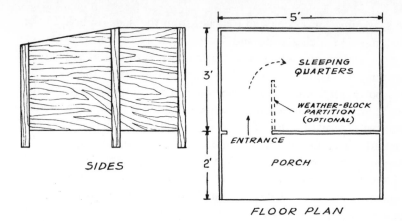

SIDES

5'

3'

SLEEPING QUARTERS

WEATHER-BLOCK PARTITION (OPTIONAL)

ENTRANCE

2'

PORCH

FLOOR PLAN

FINISHED HOUSE

E.H.H.

the back slope over the sleeping portion which will accommodate the hinged roof.

Next build the floor frame and cover it with five-eighths-inch outdoor plywood or tongue and groove siding. Cover the sides with the same material you use for the floor. If you allow your two-by-three-inch framing to show on the outside of the house, you will have a smooth inner surface to which to attach your floor platform. Keep the floor the six inches above ground level provided by your side uprights and brace the floor by nailing six-inch pieces of two by threes under the floor and to the inside bottom of the side uprights. Frame in the door section between the porch and the sleeping quarters, framing for a door 4 to 6 inches from the floor (to hold in the bedding), 18 inches wide and 2 feet high. Nail your plywood or tongue and groove siding over this framework, of course leaving the opening for the door, and nail the same wood across the back and the porch roof, thus closing the house in all around except for the roof section over the sleeping quarters. Build this section separately with an overlay of four inches on the two sides and the back. Attach an underneath flange of wood on both sides and the rear, in from the edges, so that the flanges will fit snugly along the three outside edges of the house proper to keep out drafts and cold. Hinge this roof section to the back edge of the porch roof and cover the entire roof part with shingles or heavy tar paper, with a separate ten-inch flap stripped along and covering the hinged edge. Paint the house (blue or blue-gray paint is said to discourage flies), and it is finished.

If you wish, you may insulate with board insulation on the inside; or double flooring can be provided with insulating paper between

This is a very practical dog house for your Collie. It is large, light and airy and has the added advantage of being a children's play house during the day.

Ch. Gatebeck Indelible, owned by Miss M. Lottery. Photo by C. M. Cooke.

the layers. In cold weather a gunny sack or a piece of canvas, rug or blanket, should be tacked at the top edge of the doorway to fall across the opening, thus blocking out cold air. If the house is big enough, an inside partial wall can be provided at one side of the door, essentially dividing the inner portion into a front hall with a weather-blocking partition between this hall and the sleeping quarters. If you build the house without the porch, you will find it necessary to build a separate platform on which the dog can lie outside in the sun after snow or rain. Should your ambitions embrace a full-sized kennel building with office, etc., it might be wise to investigate the prefabricated kennel buildings which are now on the market.

This house that you build, because of its size, is not an easy thing to handle or carry, so we suggest that you build it as close as possible to the site you have picked for it. The site should be at the narrow end of the run, with just a few inches of the arch jutting into the run and the greater bulk of the house outside of the run proper. Situate the house at the door end of the run, so that when you approach the run, the dog will not track through his excreta which will be distributed at the end of the run farthest from the door. Try to set the house with its side to the north and its back to the west. This gives protection from the coldest compass point in winter and shades the porch from the hot afternoon sun in summer.

A house built to the dimensions advised will accommodate two fully grown Collies comfortably if the weather-block partition is eliminated, or only one mature dog if it is not. Remember that the smaller and lower you can build your house without cramping your dog, the warmer it will be in winter. If the house is not too large, is well built, and the doorway blocked adequately, you will be surprised by the amount of heat the dog's body will generate in cold weather to keep his sleeping quarters warm. To house several dogs, the necessary number of houses can be built, or if you so wish, one house doubled in length, with a dividing partition and two doorways, to service two separate runs.

Bedding for the sleeping box can consist of marsh grass, oat, rye, or wheat straw, or wood, pine, or cedar shavings. The latter is said to discourage fleas and lice and possesses an aromatic odor. If any of the other materials are used, shake a liberal supply of flea powder into the bedding once a week or each time the bedding is changed. The bedding may be changed once a month but should be changed more often in rainy or muddy weather. Old bedding should be burned so it will not become a breeding place for parasites. Periodically, the dog house should be cleaned out, washed with soap and water and a good disinfectant, and aired with the hinged roof section propped open.

GROOMING

Grooming should be a pleasant experience and a time of silent and delightful communication between you and your dog. Try to find the time to groom your Collie once every day. It should take only a few minutes of your time, except during the season of shedding. By removing dead hair, dust, and skin scales in the daily grooming, you keep your Collie's coat glossy, his appearance neat. During the grooming procedure, beginning skin disease can be seen and nipped in the bud.

But it is not entirely necessary to brush your Collie more than twice weekly under normal conditions. Remember that your Collie

It should be part of your child's chores to comb out the knots in your Collie's coat every day. By keeping after it you'll have a healthier, handsomer dog.

is a double-coated dog. The long hairs are called guard hairs; the undercoat, which is soft and woolly, insulates the dog against both cold and heat and keeps water from soaking through to the skin. This undercoat is shed by the dog and should be completely combed out when you find that it is loose enough for you to be able to pluck it out with your hand without trouble. To accomplish this, use a metal-tooth comb gently and carefully. Sometimes a warm bath will help to expedite matters.

Of course, the easy way is to take your dog to a grooming shop or kennel and then watch how it is done so that you can do it yourself

Grooming time for a Collie is an important time. A Collie, especially a rough, soon has masses of tangles if he isn't groomed regularly. The best schedule is to brush your Collie's coat once a day. At the same time you can use some flea and tick sprays to insure that he doesn't support any parasites. Your petshop has all the items you will need to keep your Collie in the best of condition.

Grooming a Collie before showing requires only a little touching up if you have been diligent about keeping the dog groomed every day.

in the future. Be sure to use a natural bristle brush and not a nylon brush; nylon has a tendency to tear the guard hairs and leave a ragged appearance. If done correctly and about twice a week, each grooming should take approximately fifteen minutes.

BATHING

You may bathe your dog or puppy any time you think necessary, as long as it is not too frequently. Be careful in chilly weather to bathe him in a warm room and make sure he is completely dry before you allow him to venture out into the cold. When you bathe your dog, soak him down to the skin and remove the protective oils from his coat. Be careful that he is not exposed to winter conditions directly after a bath, as there is danger of his contracting a cold. During the time of shedding, a bath once a week is not too often if the weather is warm. It helps to remove loose hair and skin scales,

If certain parts of your Collie have thick accumulations of dirt, it is better to brush out the dirt before bathing him.

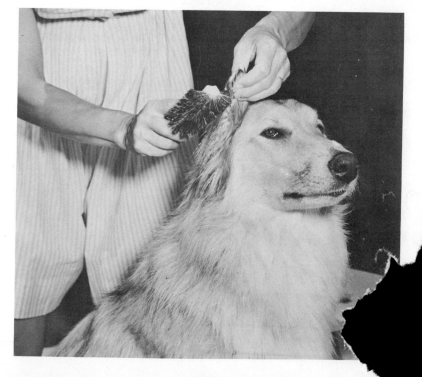

as does the grooming that should follow the bath when the dog is completely dry. As mentioned above, your dog's coat is water-resistant, so the easiest way to insure the removal of deep dirt and odors caused by accumulated sebum is by employing a chemicalized liquid soap with a coconut-oil base. Some commercial dog soaps contain vermin poisons, but an occasional prepared vermicidal dip, after bathing and rinsing, is more effective and very much worth while. When bathing, rub the lather in strongly down to the skin, being careful not to get soap in the dog's eyes. Cover every inch of him with heavy lather, rub it in, scrape the excess off with your hands, rinse and dry thoroughly, then walk him in the sun until he is ready for grooming. There are available paste soaps that require no rinsing, making the bathing of your Collie that much easier, or you may wish to use liquid detergents manufactured specifically for canine bathing. Prepared canned lathers, as well as dry shampoos, are all available at pet shops and are all useful in keeping your dog clean and odorless.

There are many people who do not believe in frequent bathing because it tends to remove the oil from the dog's coat and can result

One of the rewards for having a well trained Collie is that he will stand while you bathe him. This makes the job so much easier. Imagine fighting a Collie in a bathtub?

Rub the soap in deep to reach the skin. This Collie enjoys the 'rubbing in' part of the bath more than any other part.

Whatever soap you use be certain that it was made for dogs. The use of human soaps on dogs can only mean skin problems.

in dry skin, dandruff, and skin itch. If you are in this category and wish to keep your dog clean and fresh-looking without fully bathing him, you can do so by employing the following procedure. First, fill a pail with lukewarm water and swish a bar of a bland canine soap through the water until it is slightly cloudy. Dip a large towel in the water and throw it over your Collie's back in much the same manner as a drying blanket is draped over a horse. Begin rubbing the moisture through your dog's coat from behind his ears down his neck, back, croup, etc., until you have rubbed him all over. Then rinse the towel in fresh water, wring it out, and repeat the procedure until the first liquid application has been completely removed. Following this, rub the dog down briskly with a dry towel, comb him in the direction of the lay of his coat, and allow him to dry in the sun if possible. Do not permit him to roll in dirt or earth, a habit which seems to be the particular delight of most dogs after bathing or grooming.

If your dog has walked in tar which you find you cannot remove by bathing, you can remove it with kerosene. The kerosene should be quickly removed with strong soap and water so it will not burn and irritate the skin. Paint can be washed off with turpentine, which must also be quickly removed for the same reasons. Some synthetic paints, varnishes, enamels, and other like preparations, which are thinned with alcohol, can be removed by the same vehicle. If the paint (oil base) is close to the skin, linseed oil will dissolve it without irritation. Should your dog engage in a tête-à-tête with a skunk, wash him immediately (if you can get near him) with soap and hot water, or soak him with tomato juice if you can find enough available,

After the rinsing use a large towel to completely cover the Collie or he will shake his body so vigorously that you will end up with a shower bath.

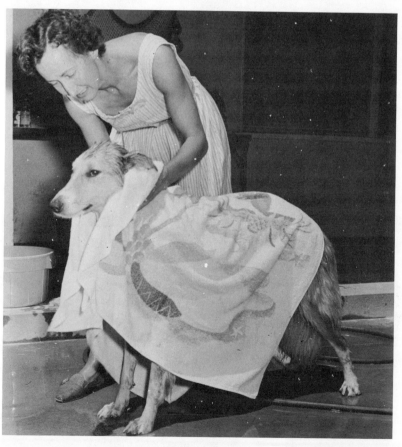

If it is a bit chilly in the air, use a hair drier to complete the drying process. If it is a warm, sunny day, your Collie can dry out in the air.

After your Collie has been thoroughly dried, give him a good brushing with a heavy brush to bring out as much of the moisture retained in his coat as possible.

then walk him in the hot sun. The odor evaporates most quickly under heat.

Small sticks with cotton-tipped ends, which are manufactured under various brand names, are excellent for cleaning your dog's ears. Drop into the ear a mixture of ether and alcohol, or of propylene glycol, to dissolve dirt and wax; then swab the ear clean with the cotton-tipped stick. Surplus liquid will quickly evaporate.

CARE OF TOENAILS AND TEETH

Keep your dog's nails trimmed short. Overgrown nails cause lameness, foot ailments, spread toes, and hare feet. If your dog does a great deal of walking on cement, nail growth is often kept under control naturally by wearing off on the cement surface. Some dogs seem to possess a genetic factor for short nails which never need

Use a special dog nail clipper to trim your Collie's nails. This special type of clipper is safer to use as it doesn't slip and you are less liable to cut into the vein running through the nail.

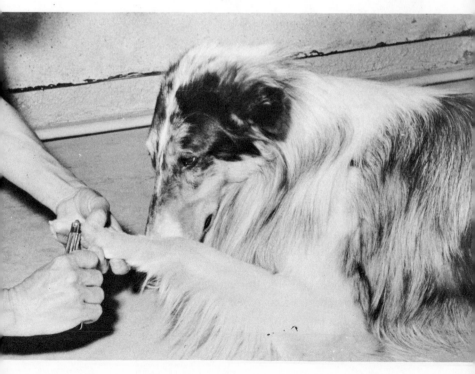

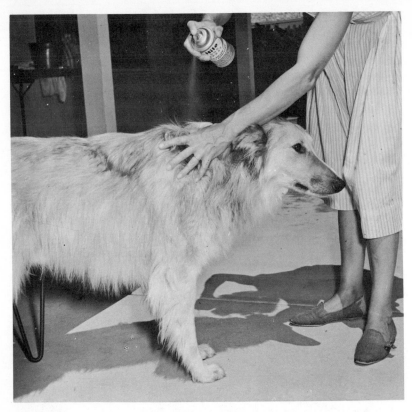

After the bath, when the Collie is completely dry, spray the dog with a flea and tick repellent in order to keep your Collie free of parasites he may pick up in the woods.

trimming, but the majority of our dogs need nail care. To accomplish this task with the least possible trouble, use a nail cutter specifically designed to trim canine nails and cut away only the horny dead section of the nail. If you cut too deeply you will cause bleeding. A flashlight held under the nail will enable you to see the dark area of the blood line so you can avoid cutting into it. If you should tap the blood supply in the nail, don't be overly alarmed; simply keep the dog quiet until the severed capillaries close and the bleeding stops. Munsel's solution or a styptic pencil applied to the bleeding nail helps to hurry coagulation. After you have cut the nails, file them smooth with the use of an ordinary carpenter's file. File from above with a downward, rounding stroke. If a nail has bled from trimming, do not file it for at least twenty-four hours.

Soft rib bones fed twice a week will help prevent tartar from forming on your dog's teeth. His teeth pierce the bones, scraping off tooth residue in the process, keeping his teeth clean and white. If tartar should form, it can be chipped off with the same kind of instrument your dentist uses on your teeth for that purpose, or your veterinarian can clean them efficiently without bother to you. Check your dog's mouth every other week for broken, loose, or abscessed teeth, particularly when he has passed his prime. Bad teeth must be tended by your veterinarian before they affect your Collie's general health.

FLIES

During the summer months certain flies, commonly called "deer" flies, bite at the tips of a dog's ears, causing great discomfort, the formation of scabs, subsequent baldness, and sometimes infection in that area. A good liquid insecticide, one of the many recently developed for fly control, should be rubbed or sprayed on the dog's ears as often as necessary to keep these pests away. Skin-disease salve which contains sulphur and oil of turpentine as a vehicle is also efficacious against flies, particularly if D.D.T. flea powder is shaken on top of the salve where it adheres, giving extra protection. Oil of Benzoin and oil of Cade painted on the ears, are also effective.

RATS

If rats invade the kennel area, they should be eradicated as quickly as possible. Not only are they disease carriers but they are an affront to our more delicate senses. To get rid of them, set out small pans of dog meal near their holes nightly for several nights until you have them coming to these pans to feed. Then mix Red Squill with the dog food they are being fed, eight measures of dog meal to one of Red Squill. After a single night's feeding of this poisonous mixture, you will generally rid your premises of these gray marauders. Red Squill is a drug that is nonpoisonous to all animals except rodents, so it can be used around the kennel with safety.

TRAVEL

When traveling with your dog in hot weather, never leave him alone in a closed car in the sun. Each summer death takes its grisly toll of dogs so treated. Carry his water pail and food dish with you

If you are in a strange place and you must stake your Collie in the open sun, keep plenty of cool water handy and cover your Collie with a damp towel once or twice during the day so he can cool off.

and take care of his needs as you do your own when on the road. If you intend changing his diet to one more easily fed when traveling, begin the change a few days before your trip so he can become accustomed to it. Gaines Research Division publishes a list of approximately 3,500 hostelries across the country that will accept dogs—a handy booklet for the dog-loving traveler to have.

If you find it necessary to ship a Collie to another section of the country, make sure the crate you use is large enough in all dimensions to keep the dog from being cramped during his journey. Check to see that there are no large openings or weak sections which might break in transit and allow the dog's limbs to project out of the crate. Consult your veterinarian or your local express agency for data on state health certificates. Supply the dog with a pan, rigidly attached to the crate, for water, and throw a few dog biscuits on the floor of the crate for the dog to gnaw during his journey to alleviate boredom. Be sure there are air holes in strategic locations to provide air and ventilation. If possible, the top surface of the crate should be rounded, rather than flat, to discourage the parking of other crates on top of the dog crate. Strips of wood, nailed horizontally along the outside of the crate and projecting out from the surface, will prevent adjacent crates, or boxes, from being jammed tightly against the dog crate and thus blocking and defeating the purpose of the ventilation holes.

A periodic health check of your dog by your veterinarian can pay big mental and monetary dividends. When you take him for his examination, remember to bring with you samples of his stool and urine for analysis.

EXERCISE

Exercise is one of the facets of canine care that is many times neglected by the owner. Dogs need a great deal more exercise than humans, so taking your dog for a walk on leash cannot be considered exercise from the canine standpoint. If you can allow him to run free when you take him out, he will get more exercise, but still just a

Old Collies never die, they just fade away! This fellow is 14 years old. He goes with the family everywhere the family goes. Keep your Collie comfortable whenever you travel. If you can't keep him comfortable, board him. Your petshop will be able to help you locate a boarding kennel if they are unable to board him for you.

A beautiful head study of Ch. Vir-Jo's Gold N'Honey, owned by Rock Dorburt Kennels.

bare modicum of what is necessary. If you teach him to chase a ball and retrieve it, he will get still more exercise, while you can take your ease. But the best way to provide a Collie with correct and substantial exercise is to train him to trot beside a bicycle. In this manner he will receive the steady movement which will give him co-ordination, muscular fluidity, and tightness.

We have considered in this chapter the elements of physical care, but we must not forget that your Collie needs mental care as well. His character and mental health need nourishment, grooming, and exercise, just as much as his physical being. Give him your companionship and understanding, teach him right from wrong, and treat him as you would a friend with whom you enjoy associating. This, too, is part of his general care, and perhaps the most important part for both you and your Collie.

Remember that good general care is the first and most important part of canine ownership and disease prevention. The health and happiness of your dog is in your hands. A small amount of labor each day by those hands is your dog's health and life insurance, and the premium is paid by your Collie in love and devotion.

7.

The Brood Bitch and the Stud

If we want to succeed in improvement within our breed, we must have an even greater trueness to breed type in our bitches than we have in their breeding partners. The productive value of the bitch is comparatively limited in scope by seasonal vagary and this, in turn, increases the importance of every litter she produces.

To begin breeding we must, of necessity, begin with a bitch as the foundation. The foundation of all things must be strong and free from faults or the structure we build upon it will crumble. The bitch we choose for our foundation bitch must, then, be a good bitch, as fine as we can possibly acquire, not in structure alone but in mentality and character as well. She is a product of her germ plasm, and this most important facet of her being must be closely analyzed so that we can compensate, in breeding, for her hidden faults. Structurally, the good brood bitch should be strongly made and up to standard size. She should be deep and not too long in body, for overlong bitches are generally too long in loin and weak in back, and after a litter tend to sag in back line. She must possess good bone strength throughout, yet she should not be so coarse as to lack femininity. Weakness and delicacy are not the essence of femininity in our breed and should be particularly avoided in the brood bitch.

Your bitch will first come in season when she is between eight and twelve months of age. Though this is an indication that nature considers her old enough and developed enough to breed, it is best to allow her to pass this first heat and plan to breed her when she next comes in season. This should come within six months if her environment remains the same. Daylight, which is thought to affect certain glands, occasionally seems to influence the ratio of time between heats, as will complete change in environment. Scientific studies of the incidence of seasonal variation in the mating cycles of bitches indicates that more bitches come in heat and are bred during the months of February through May than at any other time of year. The figures might not be completely reliable since they were assembled through birth registrations in the A.K.C., and many breeders refrain from fall and winter breedings so they will not have winter or early spring litters. Small breeds reach maturity much earlier than do our Collies, and bitches of these breeds can be bred at first heat, which generally comes at a younger age.

When your bitch is approaching her period of heat and you intend to breed her, have her stool checked for intestinal parasites, and if any are present, worm her. Feed her a well-balanced diet, such as she should have been getting all along. Her appetite will increase in the preparatory stage of the mating cycle as her vulva begins to swell. She will become restless, will urinate more frequently, and will allow dogs to approach her, but will not allow copulation. Within the bitch

Ch. Bonnydale Barbette, owned by Julia Finnegan.

other changes are taking place at this stage. Congestion begins in the reproductive tract, the horns of the uterus and the vagina thicken, and the luteal bodies leave the ovaries.

The first sign of blood from the vulva ushers in the second stage of the mating cycle. In some bitches no blood appears at all, or so little that it goes unnoticed by the owner, and sometimes we find a bitch who will bleed throughout the cycle. In either circumstance we must depend upon other signs. The bitch becomes very playful

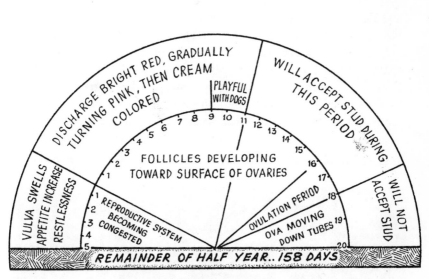

NORMAL BITCH MATING CYCLE

with animals of her own and the opposite sex but will still not permit copulation. This is, of course, a condition which is very trying to male dogs with whom she comes in contact. Congestion within the bitch reaches a high point during this period. Ova develop within the follicles of the ovaries and, normally, the red discharge gradually turns to pink, becoming lighter in color until it becomes straw color and is no longer obvious. Her vulva is more swollen and she becomes increasingly more playful with males. This period is generally of about ten days' duration, but the time varies greatly with the individual. Rather than rely upon any set time period, it is best to conclude that this period reaches its conclusion when the bitch will stand for the stud and permit copulation. This generally occurs at about the tenth day, but can take place as early as the fourth or fifth day of this period or as late as the seventeenth day.

The third period in the cycle is the acceptance period. The bitch will swing her hind end toward the dog, her tail will arch and fall to the side, and she will permit copulation. Sometimes the stud may have to tease her for a time, but she will eventually give in. The bitch may be sensitive and yelp and pull away when the stud's penis touches the lining of the vagina. If this occurs several times, it is best to wait another day until the sensitivity has left this region. A very definite indication that the bitch is in the acceptance period is the softness and flaccidity of the vulva from which the firmness and congestion has gone. Within the bitch the ovarian follicles have been growing ever bigger, and approximately midway in the acceptance period, some of them burst and the eggs are ready for fertilization. If the bitch has a normal mating cycle as shown on the diagram, the best time to breed her is about the thirteenth or fourteenth day of the mating cycle when ovulation has occurred. This time also varies with

Ch. Beulah's Silver Maravellia, owned by Mrs. N. K. George. Photo by C. M. Cooke.

Ch. Andrew of Arcot, owned by Mrs. M. J. Tweddle. Photo by C. M. Cooke.

the individual bitch, so that until you have bred your bitch once or twice and feel that you know the best time for her, it is better to breed her on the eleventh day and every other day thereafter until her period of acceptance is over. This last, of course, is generally possible only when the stud is owned by you. One good breeding is actually all that is necessary to make your bitch pregnant, providing that breeding is made at the right time. If copulation is forced before the bitch is ready, the result is no conception or a small litter, since the sperm must wait for ovulation and the life of the sperm is limited. The acceptance period ceases rather abruptly and is signaled by the bitch's definite resistance to male advances.

If your bitch is a maiden, it is best to breed her this first time to an older stud who knows his business. When you bring her to the stud and if there are adjoining wire-enclosed runs, put the stud in one run and the bitch in the adjacent one. They will make overtures through the wire and later, when the stud is loosed in the run with the bitch, copulation generally occurs quickly. You may have to hold the bitch if she is flighty or reluctant, sometimes a problem with maiden bitches. If your bitch fails to conceive from a good and proper breeding, do not immediately put the blame on the stud. In

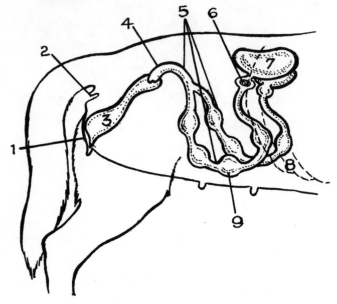

REPRODUCTION SYSTEM OF BITCH

1. Vulva. 2. Anus. 3. Vagina. 4. Cervix. 5. Uterus. 6. Ovary. 7. Kidneys. 8. Ribs. 9. Feotal lump.

most instances it is the fault of either the bitch or the owner of the bitch who has not adequately timed the mating. Many bitch owners fail to recognize the first signs of the mating cycle and so bring their bitch to the stud either too early or too late. Normal physiology of the reproductive system can be interrupted or delayed by disturbance, disease, or illness in any part of the dog's body. A sick bitch will therefore generally not come in season, though it is time to do so, until after she has completely recovered and returned to normal. Bitches past their prime and older tend to have a shorter mating cycle and so must be bred sooner than usual to assure pregnancy.

During copulation and the resulting tie, you should assist the stud dog owner as much as possible. If the stud evidences pain when he attempts to force his penis in the vulva, check the bitch. In virgin bitches you may find a web of flesh which runs vertically across the vaginal opening and causes pain to the dog when his penis is forced against it. This web must be broken by hooking your finger around it and pulling if a breeding is to be consummated. After the tense

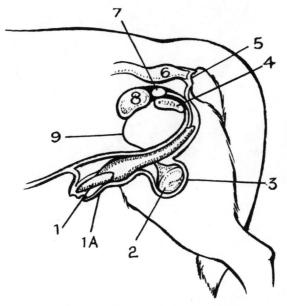

REPRODUCTION SYSTEM OF MALE

1a. Sheath. 1. Penis. 2. Testicle. 3. Scrotum. 4. Pelvic bone.
5. Anus. 6. Rectum. 7. Prostate. 8. Bladder. 9. Vas deferens.

excitement of the breeding and while the tie is in effect, speak to the bitch quietly and keep her from moving until the tie is broken, then snap a leash onto her collar and take her for a fast walk around the block without pausing. After that she can be taken home in the car. If it is necessary to travel any great distance before she arrives again in familiar surroundings, it is best to allow her a period of quiet rest before attempting the journey.

Occasionally fertile bitches, whether bred or not, will have phantom pregnancies and show every physical manifestation of true gestation up to the last moment. In some cases a bitch may be truly

The author examines a young sable male Collie before she introduces him to his mate. It is a good idea for the breeder to be familiar with both the bitch and the dog before breeding them. Here she is testing the dog to see how well trained it is to her commands before she introduces the bitch. Sometimes there can be a bit of a fight between two Collies if they reject one another for breeding purposes.

bred and then, after a month, resorb her fetuses. The only way of differentiating between pseudo-pregnancy and fetal resorbtion is by palpation, or feeling with the hands, to locate the fetal lump in the uterus. This is a difficult task for one who has not had vast experience.

After you have returned home with your bitch, do not allow any males near her. She can become impregnated by a second dog and whelp a litter of mixed paternity, some of the puppies sired by the first dog and others sired by the second animal. Often a bitch is bred to a selected stud just before ovulation. The sperm will live long enough to fertilize the eggs when they flush down. The next day another male breeds to the bitch, the sperm of the two dogs mix within her and both become sires of the resulting litter.

Let us assume that your bitch is in good health and you have had a good breeding to the stud of your choice at the proper time in the bitch's mating cycle to insure pregnancy. The male sperm fertilizes the eggs and life begins. From this moment on you will begin to feed the puppies which will be born in about sixty to sixty-three days from ovulation. Every bit of food you give the bitch is nutritionally aiding in the fetal development within her. Be sure that she is being provided with enough milk to supply calcium, meat for phosphorus and iron, and all the other essential vitamins and minerals. A vitamin and mineral supplement may be incorporated into the food if used moderately. Alfalfa leaf meal of 24 per cent protein content should become part of the diet. She must be fed well for her own maintenance and for the development of the young *in utero*, particularly during the last thirty days of the gestation period. She should not, however, be given food to such excess that she becomes fat.

Your bitch, her run, and house or bed should be free of worm and flea eggs. She should be allowed a moderate amount of free exercise in the pre-natal period to keep her from becoming fat and soft and from losing muscular tone and elasticity. If your bitch has not had enough exercise prior to breeding and you wish to harden and reduce her, accustom her to the exercise gradually and it will do her a great deal of good, but do not allow her to indulge in unaccustomed, abrupt, or violent exercise, or she might abort.

The puppies develop in the horns of the uterus, not in the "tubes" (Fallopian tubes) as is commonly thought. As the puppies develop, the horns of the uterus lengthen and the walls expand until the uterus may become as long as three and a half feet in a Collie bitch carrying a large litter. A month before the bitch is due to whelp, incorporate fresh liver in her diet two or three times a week. This helps to keep her free from constipation and aids in the coming necessary production of milk for the litter. If the litter is going to be small, she will not show much sign until late in the gestation period, but if the litter is going to be a normal or large one, she will begin to show distention of the abdomen at about thirty-five days after the breeding. Her appetite will have been increasing during this time and gradually the fact of her pregnancy will become more and more evident.

Several days before she is due to whelp, the whelping box should be prepared. It should be located in a dimly lit area removed from disturbance by other dogs or humans. The box should be four feet square, enclosed on all sides by eight to ten-inch high boards, either plank or plywood. Boards of the same height must be added above these in about three weeks to keep the pups from climbing out. Four inches up from the flooring (when it is packed down), a one by three-inch smooth wooden slat should be attached to the sides with small angle irons, all around as a rail or a pipe rail can be used. This will prevent the bitch from accidentally squeezing to death any puppy which crawls behind her. On the floor of the box lay a smooth piece of rubber matting which is easily removed and cleaned when the bedding is cleaned or changed. The bedding itself should be of rye or oat straw, and enough of it supplied so that the bitch can hollow out a nest and still leave some of the nesting material under the pups.

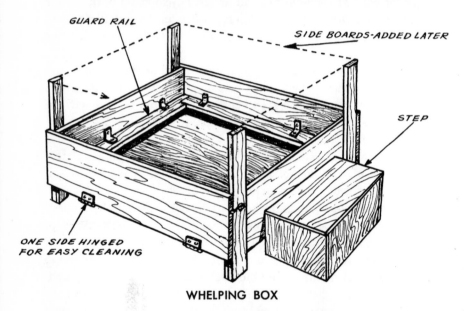

GUARD RAIL

SIDE BOARDS-ADDED LATER

STEP

ONE SIDE HINGED
FOR EASY CLEANING

WHELPING BOX

Another method much used is to have several layers of newspapers in the bottom of the box so that they can be removed one or two at a time as they become soiled during whelping. After the litter is completely whelped, the straw bedding is provided and hollowed into a saucer shape so the whelps will be kept together in a limited area. The whelping box should be raised from the ground and a smaller box, or step, provided to make it easier for the bitch to enter or leave.

As the time approaches for the whelping, the bitch will become restless; she may refuse food and begin to make her nest. Her temperature will drop approximately one degree the day before she is ready to whelp and she will show a definite dropping down through the abdomen. Labor begins with pressure from within and forces the puppies toward the pelvis. The bitch generally twists around as the puppy is being expelled to lick the fluid which accompanies the birth. Sometimes the sac surrounding the puppy will burst from pressure. If it doesn't, the puppy will be born in the sac, a thin, membranous material called the fetal envelope. The navel cord runs from the puppy's navel to the afterbirth, or placenta. If the bitch is left alone at whelping time, she will rip the fetal caul, bite off the navel cord and eat the sac, cord, and placenta. Should the cord be broken off in birth so that the placenta remains in the bitch, it will generally be expelled with the birth of the next whelp. After disposing of these items, the bitch will lick and clean the new puppy until the next one is about to be born, and the process will then repeat itself. Under completely normal circumstances, your Collie bitch is quite able to whelp her litter and look after it without any help from you, but since the whelping might not be normal, it is best for the breeder

Int. Ch. Riffelsee Regality of Dunsinane, owned by Mrs. A. F. Chatfield. Photo by C. M. Cooke.

to be present, particularly so in the case of bitches who are having their first litter.

If the breeder is present, he or she can remove the sac, cut the umbilical cord, and gently pull on the rest of the cord, assuming that the placenta has not yet been ejected, until it is detached and drawn out. Some breeders keep a small box handy in which they place each placenta, so they can, when the whelping is completed, check it against the number of puppies to make sure that no placenta has been retained. The navel cord should be cut about three inches from the pup's belly. The surplus will dry up and drop off in a few days. There is no need to tie it after cutting. You need not attempt to sterilize your hands or the implements you might use in helping the bitch to whelp, since the pups will be practically surrounded with bacteria of all kinds, some benign and others which they are born equipped to combat.

If a bitch seems to be having difficulty in expelling a particularly large puppy, you can help by wrapping a towel around your hands to give you purchase, grasping the partly expelled whelp, and pulling

By lining the whelping box with clean newspapers, you can save yourself a messy job of cleaning up if there happens to be some blood lost during the whelping time.

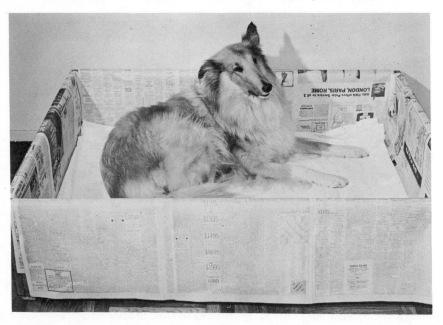

Ch. Coronation Powder Smoke, owned by Isabel Chamberlin. Photo by Evelyn M. Shafer.

gently. Do not pull too hard or you might injure the pup. The puppies can be born either head first or tail first. Either way is normal. As the pups are born, the sac broken, and the cord snipped, dry them gently but vigorously with a towel and put them at the mother's breast, first squeezing some milk to the surface and then opening their mouths for the entrance of the teat. You may have to hold them there by the head until they begin sucking.

Often several puppies are born in rapid succession, then an interval of time may elapse before another one is born. If the bitch is a slow whelper and seems to be laboring hard after one or more pups have been born, regular injections of Pitocin, at three-hour intervals, using a little less than one-half c.c., can help her in delivery. Pituitrin, one-half to one c.c., is a similar drug and the one most often used, though Pitocin brings less nausea and directly affects the uterus. Both these drugs should be administered hypodermically into the hind leg of the bitch at the rear of the thigh. After the bitch has seemingly completed her whelping, it is good practice to administer another shot of the drug to make sure no last pup, alive or dead, is

Sometimes a pup doesn't get enough feeding from its mother and additional help is necessary in the form of a baby bottle with 'formula.' Keep your eye on the pups to be sure that they are all feeding properly.

still unborn and to cause her to clean out any residue left from the whelping. Never use either of these drugs until she has whelped at least one pup.

Allow her to rest quietly and enjoy the new sensation of motherhood for several hours, then insist that she leave her litter, though she won't want to, and take her out to relieve herself. Offer her some warm milk. From then on, feed her as recommended during the gestation period, with the addition of three milk feedings per day. Sometimes milk appears in the udders before birth, but generally it comes in when the pups begin to nurse, since it is manufactured by glands, from blood, while the pups are at the breast.

Now is the time to cull the litter. Of course, all young which are not normal should be culled immediately at birth. If the bitch whelps six or less pups and all seem strong and healthy, no culling is required. If she has a particularly large litter, it does not pay, in the long run, to raise all the whelps. Allow her to keep six or seven of the best and sturdiest and cull the rest. Those which you have retained will grow better and be larger and stronger than if you allowed the entire large litter to live. Quiet puppies are healthy ones. Constant crying and squirming of the pups is a danger signal, and a check should be made to see what ails them. It may be that the bitch is not providing enough milk and they are hungry, or perhaps they are cold. Sometimes the trouble is parasitic infection, or possibly coccidiosis, or navel infection. Dr. Walter Koch, in 1950, at the University of Munich, Animal Institute, reported a bacillus, Aerogenes, which he claimed caused many deaths of young puppies. This bacillus infects from contact with the dam's rectum. It multiplies rapidly in the whelp's intestines and the normal bacillus in the stomach and intestines seems to have no effect on the lethal bacillus. It begins with the first digestion of the pups and attacks the basic internal organs, exhibiting symptoms on the second or third day following birth. The pups develop cramps, fail to suck, whimper, and die within two or three days. The disease does not seem to be contagious to other well puppies. If there is something wrong with the pups, whatever it may be, you need professional advice and should call your veterinarian immediately.

What greater pleasure for an owner and a good Collie bitch, than a beautiful litter? There is great variety in the color of this litter.

Except for the removal of dew claws on the hind legs, the pups, if healthy, need not be bothered until it is time to begin their supplementary feeding at about three weeks. Dew claws should be removed on about the second day after birth. Puppies and their needs, dietary and otherwise, are discussed more fully in the chapter which follows.

There are several ills which might befall the bitch during gestation and whelping which must be considered. Eclampsia, sometimes called milk fever, is perhaps most common. This is a metabolic disturbance brought on by a deficiency of calcium and phosphorus in the diet. If you give your bitch plenty of milk and a good diet such as we have recommended, she should not be troubled with this condition. Should your bitch develop eclampsia—evidenced by troubled shaking, wild expression, muscular rigidity, and a high temperature—it can be quickly relieved by an injection of calcium gluconate in the vein.

Should your bitch be bred by accident to an undesirable animal, your veterinarian can cause her to abort by the use of any one of several efficient canine abortifacients. He can also aid old bitches

Except for the removal of dew claws, Collie pups need little medical care if they are fed properly and groomed daily. Though you can't count them all, this litter had 12 puppies in it!

who have been resorbing their fetuses to carry them full term and whelp with the aid of stilbestrol.

Mastitis, an udder infection, is a chief cause of puppy deaths. It is generally mistaken by the uninformed for "acid milk," a condition which does not exist in dogs because the bitch's milk is naturally acid. Mastitis is an udder infection which cuts off part of the milk supply and the whelps either die of infection, contracted from the infected milk, or from starvation, due to the lack of sufficient milk. It is not necessary to massage the dam's breasts at weaning time with camphorated oil. They will cake naturally and quickly quit secreting milk if left completely alone.

Growths, infections, injuries, cysts, and other and various ailments can effect the female reproductive system and must be taken care of by your veterinarian. The great majority of bitches who have been well cared for and well fed are strong and healthy, and the bearing of litters is a natural procedure—the normal function of the female to bear and rear the next generation, and in so doing fulfill her precious destiny.

THE STUD DOG

If what we have said above about the unrivaled importance of the brood bitch is true, it may be difficult to understand why we pay so much attention to the male lines of descent. The reason is that stud dogs tend to mold the aspects of the breed on the whole and in any given country, or locality, to a much greater extent than do brood bitches. While the brood bitch may control type in a kennel, the stud dog can control type over a much larger area. The truth of this can be ascertained by the application of simple mathematics.

Let us assume that the average litter is comprised of five puppies. The brood bitch will produce, then, a maximum of ten puppies a year. In that same year a popular, good producing, well-publicized stud dog may be used on the average of three times weekly (many name studs, in various breeds, have been used even more frequently over a period of several years). This popular stud can sire fifteen puppies a week, employing the figures mentioned above, or 780 puppies a year. Compare this total to the bitch's yearly total of ten puppies, and you can readily see why any one stud dog wields a much greater influence over the breed in general than does a specific brood bitch.

The care of the stud dog follows the same procedure as outlined in the chapter on general care. He needs a balanced diet, clean quarters, and plenty of exercise, but no special care as does the brood bitch. Though it is against most of the advice previously written on the subject, we recommend that the stud be used in breeding for the first time when he is about twelve months old. He is as capable of siring a litter of fine and healthy pups at this age as he ever will be. He should be bred to a steady, knowing bitch who has been bred before, and when she is entirely ready to accept him. Aid him if necessary this first time. See that nothing disturbs him during copulation. In fact, the object of this initial breeding is to see that all goes smoothly and easily. If you succeed in this aim, the young dog will be a willing and eager stud for the rest of his life, the kind of stud that is a pleasure to own and use.

American and Canadian Ch. Stoneykirk Reflection. Photo by Evelyn M. Shafer.

Ch. Peterblue Heatherette, owned by Miss K. Alexander and Miss E. Dundas Monat. Photo by C. M. Cooke.

After this first breeding, use him sparingly until he has reached sixteen or seventeen months of age. After that, if he is in good health, there is no reason why he cannot be used at least once a week or more often during his best and most fertile years.

The male organs vital for reproduction consist of a pair each of: testicles, where the sperm is produced; epididymis, in which the sperm are stored; and *vas deferens*, through which the sperm are transported. The dog possesses no seminal vesicle as does man. But, like man, the male dog is always in an active stage of reproduction and can be used at any time.

When the stud has played with the bitch for a short period and the bitch is ready, he will cover her. There is a bone in his penis, and behind this bone is a group of very sensitive nerves which cause a violent thrust reflex when pressure is applied. His penis, unlike most other animals', has a bulbous enlargement at its base. When the penis is thrust into the bitch's vagina, it goes through a muscular ring at the opening of the vagina. As it passes into the vagina, pressure on the reflex nerves causes a violent thrust forward, and the penis, and particularly the bulb, swells enormously, preventing withdrawal through the constriction band of the vulva. The stud ejaculates semen swarming with sperm, which is forced through the cervix, uterus, Fallopian tubes, and into the capsule which surrounds the ovaries, and the breeding is consummated.

The dog and bitch are tied, or "hung," and the active part of the breeding is completed. The owner of the bitch should then stand at her head and hold her by the collar. The stud's owner should kneel next to the animals with his arm or knee under the bitch's stomach, directly in front of her hindquarters, to prevent her from suddenly sitting while still tied. He should talk soothingly to the stud and gently prevent him from attempting to leave the bitch for a little while. Presently the stud owner should turn the dog around off the bitch's back by first lifting the front legs off and to the ground and then lifting one hind leg over the back of the bitch until dog and bitch are standing tail to tail.

Paladins Black Gold, owned by Thelma Brown.

Ch. Bellhaven's At Last.

Ch. Bellhaven's Liberation.

Can. Ch. Sandamac's Sandot, owned by Edward and Mildred Horton.

Dogs remain in this position for various lengths of time after copulation, but fifteen minutes to a half an hour is generally average. When the congestion of blood leaves the penis, the bulb shrinks and the animals part.

The stud dog owner should keep a muzzle handy to be used on snappy bitches. Many bitches, due to temperament, environment, or fright, may cause injury to the stud by biting. If she shows any indication of such conduct, she should be muzzled. Should she continue to attempt to bite for any length of time, it is generally because it is either too early or too late in the estrum cycle to consummate a breeding. If the bitch is small, sinks down when mounted or won't stand, she must be held up. In some instances her owner or the stud's owner will have to kneel next to her and, with his hand under and between her hind legs, push the vulva up toward the dog's penis or guide the stud's penis into her vulva. Straw or earth, pushed under her hind legs to elevate her rear quarters, is effective in the case of a bitch who is very much too small for the stud.

There is not much more that can be written about the stud, except to caution the stud owner to be careful of using drugs or injections to make his dog eager to mate or more fertile. The number of puppies born in any litter is not dependent upon the healthy and fertile male's sperm, but upon the number of eggs the bitch gives off. Should your dog prove sterile, look for basic causes first. If there seems to be no physical reason for his sterility, then a series of injections by your veterinarian (perhaps of A-P-L, anterior-pituitary-like injections) might prove efficacious.

It is often a good idea to feed the dog a light meal before he is used, particularly if he is a reluctant stud. Young or virgin studs often regurgitate due to excitement, but it does them no harm. After the tie has broken, allow both dog and bitch to drink moderately.

American and Canadian Ch. Sandamac's Mr. Sandaman, awarded the "Best in the West" for 1961 by the Collie and Shetland Sheepdog Review. Owned by Edward and Mildred Horton.

8.
Your Collie Puppy

The birth of a litter has been covered in the previous chapter on the brood bitch. As we indicated in that discussion, barring accident or complications at birth, there is little you can do for your Collie puppies until they are approximately three weeks old. At that age supplementary feedings begin. But suppose that for one reason or another the mother must be taken from her brood: what care must be given to these babies if they are to survive ? Puppies need warmth. This is provided partly by their instinctive habit of gathering together in the nest, but to a much greater extent by the warmth of the mother's body. If the mother must be taken from the nest, this extra warmth can be provided by an ordinary light bulb, or, better still, an infra-red bulb hung directly over the brood in the enclosed nest box.

By far the most important requirement of these newborn pups is proper food. Puppies are belly and instinct and nothing much more. They must be fed well and frequently. What shall we feed them, what formula can we arrive at that most closely approaches the natural milk of the mother, which we know is best ? There are prepared modified milks for orphan puppies which are commercially available and very worth while, or you can mix your own formula of ingredients which will most closely simulate natural bitch's milk. To do this, you must first know the basic quality of the dam's milk. Bitches' milk is comparatively acid; it contains less sugar and water, more ash and protein, and far more fat than cow or human milk, so we must modify our formula to conform to these differences.

To begin, purchase a can of Nestlé's Pelargon, a spray-dried, acidified, and homogenized modified milk product. If you can't get Pelargon, try any of the spray-dried baby milks, but Pelargon is best since it is, like bitches' milk, slightly acid and rich in necessary nutritive substances. To one ounce of the modified milk product, add one ounce of fresh cream. Pour six ounces of water by volume into this mixture and blend with an electric mixer or egg beater until

Three pups in a litter . . . all different.

it is smooth. Larger amounts can be mixed employing the same basic proportions and kept refrigerated. This formula should be fed five or six times a day and when fed, must be warmed to body heat. Many puppies refuse to drink a formula that has not been warmed to just the right temperature. Do not add lime water, glucose, or dextrose to the formula, for by so doing you are modifying in the wrong direction. An ordinary baby's bottle and nipple are adequate as the formula vehicle. Never drop liquids directly in the puppy's throat with an eye dropper or you invite pneumonia. A twelve-ounce puppy will absorb one ounce of formula; a one-pound puppy, approximately one and three-quarter ounces of formula; a two-pound puppy, two ounces; and a three-pound puppy, two and three-quarter ounces at each feeding. A valuable adjunct to the puppy's diet, whether formula or breast fed, is two drops of Dietol, dropped into the lip pocket from the first day of birth on, the amount to be increased with greater growth and age. A bottle trough can be built for orphan pups. The trick here is to space the nipple holes so that the bodies of the pups touch when drinking.

If it is possible to find a foster mother for orphan pups, your troubles are over. Most lactating bitches will readily take to puppies other than their own if the new babies are first prepared by spreading some of the foster mother's milk over their tiny bodies. The foster mother will lick them clean and welcome them to the nest.

When the pups are $2\frac{1}{2}$ to 3 weeks old, the mother will often engage in an action which might prove slightly disgusting to the neophyte but which is an instinctive and natural performance to the bitch. She will regurgitate her own stomach contents of partially-digested food for her puppies to eat, thus beginning, in her own way, the weaning process. If you have begun supplementary feeding in time, this action by the bitch will seldom occur. If you haven't, it is a definite indication that supplementary feeding should begin at once.

Puppies grow best on milk, meat, fat, and cereal diets. Growth is attained through proteins, but proteins differ, so that puppies fed on vegetable protein diets will not grow and thrive as well as those fed on animal proteins. Vitamins E and K (found in alfalfa meal) are essential to the pup's well being and should be used in adequate amounts in the food ration. Remember that 70 per cent of the pup's energy is derived from fat intake, so supply this food element generously in the diet. Lime water should not be incorporated in the diet since it neutralizes stomach acidity, a condition which is necessary to the assimilation of fat. In experiments, puppies on fat-free diets developed deficiency symptoms characterized by anemia, weight loss,

A litter can all look alike, as these nine sable Collie pups.

Train your Collie puppy at an early age to get along with any other pet animals that might be in the same household. It is not true that dogs and cats are natural enemies. Many Collies live in peace with cats and other animals.

dull coats, and finally death. Fat alone could not cure the advanced manifestation of the condition, indicating that some metabolic process was disturbed when complete fat removal in the diet was resorted to. But feeding butterfat plus folacin resulted in dramatic cures.

To begin the small puppy on supplementary feeding, place the pan of food before him, gently grasp his head behind the ears, and dip his lips and chin into the food. The puppy will lick his lips, taste the food, and in no time at all learn to feed by himself. Be careful not to push the head in so far that the pup's nose is covered and clogged by food.

Check the puppies' navels every day to see that infection has not set in. This infection comes from the scraping of their soft bellies on a rough surface and can generally be avoided if several thicknesses of cloth cover the floor of the nest box under the bedding.

Clip the sharp little nails to avoid damage to litter mates' eyes, which will open at about ten days. If the pups are born with hind dew

Check your Collie puppy's pedigree BEFORE you buy him.

claws, cut them off with manicure scissors about two days after birth. They need not be bandaged as the bitch will keep the wound clean until it has healed. Have a fecal check made when the pups are about $3\frac{1}{2}$ weeks old. If they are infested with worms, worm them immediately. Do not attempt to build up the pups first if the parasitic infestation has made them unthrifty. It is best to rid them of the worms quickly, after which they will speedily return to normal health and plumpness.

The weeks fly by, and before you know it the puppies are of saleable age. The breeder, you can be sure, has not wasted these weeks. He has spent many hours in close observation of the litter and has centered his interest on the one pup which he thinks shows the most promise. Either he will hold this pup for himself, sell him to a show-conscious buyer, or keep the puppy and sell it at a higher price when it has become more fully developed and its early promise becomes a fact. The strange part about this whole business of picking a young puppy from a litter is that the novice buyer many times stands as good a chance of picking the best pup as the seasoned and experienced breeder. The reason for this seeming incongruity lies in the fact that in every litter there will be *several* pups which, if well bred and well cared for, appear to be potential winners at eight to ten weeks of age. Another reason concerns the ratio of sectional growth in young animals. Each pup will have an individual growth rate and exhibit change in relative sections of the body, as well as in over-all growth, from day to day.

If you are the potential purchaser of a Collie puppy, or a grown dog for that matter, prepare yourself for the purchase first by attending as many shows as possible. Observe, absorb, and listen. Visit kennels which have well-bred, winning stock, and at shows and kennels make an unholy nuisance of yourself by asking innumerable questions of Collie people who have proven, by their record in the breed, that information gleaned from them can be respected. When you intend to purchase a new car, or an electrical appliance such as a refrigerator or washing machine, you go to sales rooms and examine the different makes, weighing their features and quality, one against the other. You inquire of friends who have different brands their opinions with regard to the utility value of the item, and, when you have made

The difference between a pet-quality Collie and a show-quality Collie has nothing to do with it being a sweet, lovable animal. You pay for the 'blood' lines and its potential to be a champion when you buy a show-quality puppy.

up your mind which brand is best, you make sure that you purchase the item from a reliable distributor. Do the same thing when you intend to purchase a dog. Before you make your journey to any breeder to buy a puppy, be sure to inquire first into the background of the breeder as well as the background of his dogs. What does this breeder actually know about his breed? What has he formerly produced? What is his reputation amongst other reputable breeders? Does his stock have balanced minds as well as balanced bodies? Find the answers to these questions even before you delve into the ancestry of the puppies he has for sale. If the answers prove that this breeder is an honest, dependable person with more than a smattering knowledge of the breed, and that he has consistently bred typical stock, then your next step will be to study the breeding of his puppies to determine whether they have been bred from worth-while stock which comes from good producing strains. Examine stock he has sold from different breedings to other customers. Be careful of kennels which are puppy factories, breeding solely for commercial reasons, and don't be carried away by hysterical, overdone, adjective-happy advertisements.

When you have satisfied yourself that the breeder is a morally responsible person who has good stock, then you may sally forth to purchase your future champion. It is best, if possible, to invite an experienced breeder to accompany you on your mission. As mentioned before, even the most experienced breeder cannot, with assurance, pick the pup in the litter which will mature into the best specimen. An experienced person can, however, keep you from selecting a very engaging youngster which exhibits obvious faults which quite possibly won't improve.

Assuming that the litter from which you are going to select your puppy is a fat and healthy one and it is a male puppy you have set your heart on having, ask the breeder to separate the sexes so you can examine the male pups only. Normal puppies are friendly, lovable creatures wanting immediate attention, so the little fellow who backs away from you and runs away and hides should be eliminated from consideration immediately. This also applies to the pup which sulks in a corner and wants no part of the proceedings. Watch the puppies from a distance of approximately twenty feet as they play and frolic, sometimes trotting and occasionally quitting their play for a fleeting moment to stand gazing at something of interest which has, for that second, engaged their attention. Don't be rushed. Take all the time

This is the proper way to hold a Collie puppy.

Take your Collie puppy outside in the daylight before you buy him and examine him when he is tied out to a stake. Make sure he is active and not crippled. Be sure that he is friendly and wants to come to someone (some dogs are shy and they are not suitable as pets). A happy, healthy Collie puppy is about the most precious thing in the world. Who said you couldn't buy love? You certainly can buy puppy love!

necessary to pick the puppy you want. You are about to pay cold cash for a companion and a dependent who will be with you for many years.

If you have been lucky enough to have had the opportunity of examining both sire and dam, determine which puppies exhibit the faults of the parents or the strain. If any particular fault seems to be overdone in a specific pup, discard him from further consideration. Do not handle the pups during this preliminary examination. Look for over-all balance first and the absence of glaring structural faults. Shy or frightened puppies (and grown dogs) have a tendency to crouch a bit, giving the illusion of beautiful hindquarter angulation, where the bold dog who possesses equal angulation will appear straighter behind. Watch the pup's movement when at trot. A good one moves with balance and lightness even though clumsy at this early age. From a uniform litter it is difficult to fully evaluate the quality and pick the best pup. Certain strains mature early while others mature slowly, improving with age.

Look for a short, straight back, not roached or swayed. The ribs should be deep, well-sprung and reaching far back, leaving a short, strong loin. The pup should be broad across the back and over the loin and croup, and the croup itself long and gently sloping to the set-on of tail, which is moderately long with a slight upward curve at

Rock Dorburt Resolute as a puppy. Note the magnificent head.

the end. The feet of a good Collie puppy should be compact and not as large and clumsy as is found in many other puppies or breeds in its size category. Avoid that novice's delight, the biggest, loosest and clumsiest pup in the litter. It will often retain its clumsiness and mature into a coarse animal. Quality of coat is important in the Rough Collie. It should not be soft, open or curly but should present a

Kittridge Indian Summer as a puppy. This magnificent pup is only 14 weeks old.

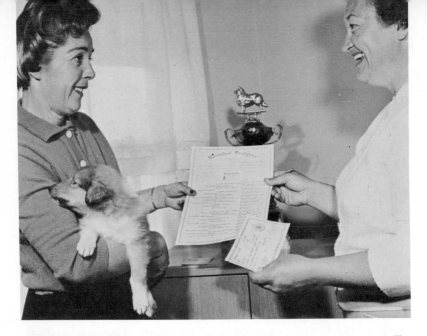

There is a great difference between a 'pedigree paper' and a 'registration paper'. The pedigree form is usually a large form giving details of the last few generations of your Collie pup. The registration form is an official Kennel Club form which certifies that the dog is a true Collie, no mixed blood, and you in turn can breed the dog and use the paper to prove its ancestry, thus enabling you to register the offspring of your pup if its mate also has been registered as a Collie.

straight, harsh appearance. Coat quality in the Collie puppy is difficult for the neophyte to determine accurately.

The head of the Collie has great importance. It should be shaped like a long, lean wedge and should not, even in the puppy phase, appear large or massive. Small ears should be selected for. Large, heavy ears never attain the correct lift or "break". Look for a clear, bright, medium-sized almond-shaped eye, dark brown in color (Blue Merles can have China eyes though the dark eye is preferred).

By this time you have probably narrowed the field down to one or two pups. It is time now to hand examine the one or two youngsters who look the best to you. Stand each one upon a table individually in a show stance, then examine the mouth for tooth and jaw structure to determine the bite. In Collies, an overshot pup frequently levels off with growth if it is not an hereditary anomaly and is slight; but an undershot jaw seldom corrects itself to any great extent by maturity. Next, attempt to determine if the pup is sexually whole.

At this age the testicles are descended into the scrotum but are often drawn up when the puppy is being handled, making it difficult to locate both testicles during examination. The buyer should have a written agreement with the seller to the effect that, should the pup prove to be a monorchid, or cryptorchid, the puppy can be returned and the purchase price refunded or the pup replaced by another of equal value.

If it is a female pup you want, look for the same values as outlined above in choosing a male. You would not, of course, go through the performance of determining sex as mentioned above. Female puppies are generally slightly smaller and show a degree of greater refinement than the males.

Remember that no one can pick a champion at eight weeks and no breeder can truthfully sell you a future winner at that age. All a

The Collie puppy is a lovable ball of fun, but he needs a lot of help to develop into this great breed we know as Collies. Love and affection are no substitute for essential foods, grooming and medical care, but add love and affection to these essentials and you are sure to be a satisfied Collie-owner with a good dog.

breeder can guarantee is the health and breeding of the puppy, and the fact that he possesses the normal complement of eyes, ears and legs. The best you can do if you are observant, knowledgeable, and lucky, is to pick the best pup in that particular litter at that particular time.

If it is at all possible, it is best to purchase two pups at the same time. They furnish company for each other, eliminate lonesome serenades during the first few nights, and are competition at the food pan. If you bring home only one pup, provide him with a stuffed dog or doll in his sleeping box which you have taken to the breeder's with you and rubbed in the nest box. This will frequently give the puppy some sense of comfort and companionship and alleviate lonesomeness that brings on dismal howling during the first night in his new home. A ticking alarm clock near the pup's bed will sometimes have the same effect.

In his new home, amidst strange surroundings, the pup will very often go off his feed for a time. This should not unduly alarm you unless his refusal to eat lasts so long that he becomes emaciated. If this occurs, ask your veterinarian for a good tonic, or change diets to tempt his palate. Never coax him or resort to forced feeding, or you will immediately spoil your pup and be a slave to him and his aggravating eating habits from that time forward. If he eats only one or two meals a day, instead of the several feedings he should have, he will survive until his appetite improves if he is otherwise healthy and vigorous. Should you find after a reasonable time and much scheming and effort that you have a naturally finicky eater, you must resign yourself to the fact that you have acquired a headache which can last for the duration of your dog's life and one which cannot be cured by aspirin. Only heroic measures can help you conquer this difficulty and you must steel yourself and cast out pity if you are to succeed. He must be starved, but really starved, until he has reached a point where dry bread resembles the most succulent beef. Only by such drastic measures can a finicky eater be cured. Dogs who have the competition of other dogs, or even a cat at the feed pan, usually display a normal appetite. For this reason it is sometimes smart for the one-dog owner to borrow a friend's or neighbor's pet to feed with his own until such time as his own dog has acquired a healthful and adequate appetite.

Arrange for your pup to have lots of sleep, particularly after feeding, a difficult chore when there are youngsters in the home, but never-

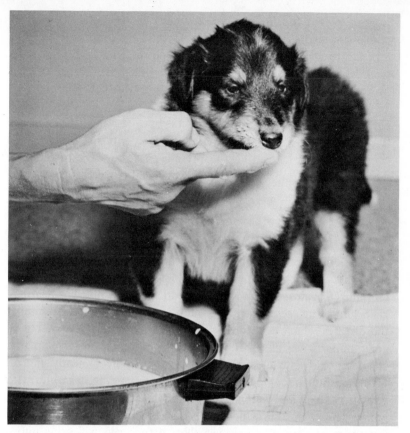

Introduce your Collie puppy to milk by allowing him to lap some from your finger. In a short time he'll be a real "chow hound."

theless very necessary to the well being of the pup. Make him feel at home so he will respond quickly to his new surroundings. It so often happens that a puppy retained by the breeder surpasses at maturity the purchased pup who was a better specimen in the beginning. This confounds the novice, yet has a reasonably simple explanation. The retained pup had no change in environment which would affect his appetite and well being during the critical period of growth, while the bought pup had and so was outstripped by his lesser litter brother.

Your puppy will have two sets of teeth; the milk teeth, which will have fallen out by the time he is approximately six months of age, and the permanent teeth, which he'll retain for the rest of his life.

Loss of weight and fever may accompany the eruption of the new, permanent teeth, but is no cause for alarm. Anatomists have a simple formula to represent the number and arrangement of permanent teeth which, at a glance, will allow you to determine if your dog has his full complement of teeth, and if he hasn't, which ones are missing. In the chart below, the horizontal line represents the division between upper and lower jaw. We begin with the incisors in the front of the dog's mouth and designate them with the letter I. The canine teeth are labeled C, the premolars, P, and the molars, M. The complete formula for a dog possessing all his teeth would be:

$$I \frac{3+3}{3+3} + C \frac{1+1}{1+1} + P \frac{4+4}{4+4} + M \frac{2+2}{3+3} = 42 \text{ teeth} \begin{array}{l} \text{(20 in upper jaw)} \\ \text{(22 in lower jaw)} \end{array}$$

Occasionally puppies develop lip warts which will disappear in a short time, leaving no aftereffects. Remember to have your puppy immunized against distemper and hepatitis and, as much as possible, keep him away from other dogs until he is old enough to combat the diseases which take their toll of the very young. Lastly, but of great importance, give your pup the opportunity to develop that character and intelligence for which the Collie is justly famed. Give him human companionship and understanding, take him with you in the car and amongst strangers. Let him live the normal, happy, and useful life which is his heritage and that tiny bundle of fur which you brought home so short a time ago will grow into a canine citizen of whom you will be proud to say, "He's mine."

9.

Fundamental Training

Responsibility for the reputation of any breed is shared by everyone who owns a specimen of that breed. Reputation, good or bad, is achieved by conduct, and conduct is the result of the molding, through training, of inherent character into specific channels of behavior.

It is a distinct pleasure to novice, old-timer, or the public at large, to watch dogs perform when they have been trained to special tasks. Here is the ultimate, the end result of the relationship between man and dog. After watching an inspired demonstration, we sometimes wonder if, under a proper training regime, our own Collie could do as well. Perhaps he can if he is temperamentally fitted for the task we have in mind. No single individual of any breed, regardless of breed type, temperament, and inheritance, is fitted to cope with all the branches of specialized service. Nor does every owner possess the qualifications or experience necessary to train dogs successfully to arduous tasks. But every dog can be trained in the fundamentals of decent behavior and every dog owner can give his dog this basic training. It is, indeed, the duty of every dog owner to teach his dog obedience to command as well as the necessary fundamentals of training which insure good conduct and gentlemanly deportment. A dog that is uncontrolled can become a nuisance and even a menace. This dog brings grief to his owner and bad reputation to himself and the breed he represents.

We cannot attempt, in this limited space, to write a complete and comprehensive treatise on all the aspects of dog training. There are several worthwhile books, written by experienced trainers, that cover the entire varied field of initial and advanced training. There are, furthermore, hundreds of training classes throughout the country where both the dog and its owner can receive standard obedience training for a nominal fee, under the guidance of experienced trainers. Here in these pages you will find only specific suggestions on some points of simple basic training which we feel are neglected in most of the books on this subject. We will also attempt to give you basic reasons for training techniques and explain natural limitations to aid you in eliminating future, perhaps drastic, mistakes.

The key to all canine training, simple or advanced, is control. Once you have established control over your Collie, you can, if you so desire, progress to advanced or specialized training in any field. The dog's only boundaries to learning are his own basic limitations. This vital control must be established during the basic training in good manners.

Almost every Collie is responsive to training. He loves his master and finds delight in pleasing him. To approach the training problem with your Collie, to make it a pleasant and easy intimacy rather than an arduous and wearisome task, you must first learn a few fundamentals. In the preceding paragraph we spoke of control as the paramount essential to training. To gain control over your dog, you must first establish control over your own vagaries of temperament. During training, when you lose your temper, you lose control. Shouting, nagging repetition, angry reprimand, and exasperation only confuse your canine pupil. If he does not obey, then the lesson has not been learned. He needs teaching, not punishment. The time of training should be approached with pleasure by both master and dog, so that both you and your pupil will look forward to these periods of contact. If you establish this atmosphere your dog will enjoy working, and a dog who enjoys his work, who is constantly trying to please, is a dog who is always under control.

Consistency is the brother of control in training. Perform each movement used in schooling in the same manner every time. Use the same words of command or communication without variance. Employ command words that are single simple, syllables, chosen for their crispness and difference in sound. Don't call your dog to you one day with the command, "Come," and the next day, with the command, "Here," and expect the animal to understand and perform the act with alacrity. Inconsistency will confuse your dog. If you are inconsistent, the dog will not perform correctly and your control is lost. By consistency you establish habit patterns which eventually become an inherent part of your Collie's behavior. Remember that a few simple commands, well learned, are much better than many and varied commands only partially absorbed. Therefore be certain that your dog understands a command completely and will perform

It takes training to have your Collie get along peacefully with this cat. Training is important in the life of your Collie . . . and the life of the household. A Collie without training is an animal. A trained Collie is a pet. Do you want an animal or a pet in your life?

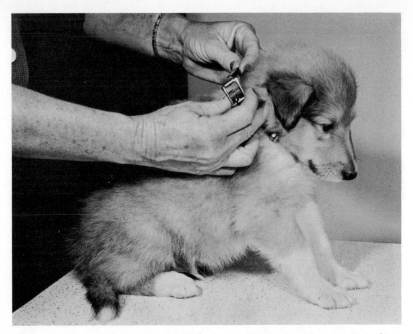

One of the first steps in training your Collie puppy is to introduce him to his first collar.

the action it demands quickly and without hesitation before attempting to teach him a new command.

Before we begin training we must first assess our prospective pupil's intelligence and character. We must understand that his eyesight is not as keen as ours, but that he is quick to notice movement. We must know that sound and scent are his chief means of communication with his world and that in these departments he is far superior to us. We must reach him, then, through voice and gesture and realize that he is very sensitive to quality change and intonation of the commanding voice. Therefore, any given command must have a definite tonal value in keeping with its purpose. The word "no" used in reprimand must be expressed sharply and with overtones of displeasure, while "good boy," employed as praise, should be spoken lightly and pleasantly. In early training the puppy recognizes distinctive sound coupled with the quality of tone used rather than individual words.

All words of positive command should be spoken sharply and distinctly during training. By this we do not mean that commands must be shouted, a practice which seems to be gaining favor in obedience work and which is very much to be deplored. A well-trained, mature Collie can be kept completely under control and will obey quickly and willingly when commands are given in an ordinary conversational tone. The first word a puppy learns is the word-sound of his name; therefore, in training, his name should be spoken first to attract his attention to the command which follows. Thus, when we want our dog to come to us, and his name is Prince, we command, "Prince! Come!"

Intelligence varies in dogs as it does in all animals, human or otherwise. The ability to learn and to perform is limited by intelligence, facets of character, and structure, such as willingness, energy, sensitivity, agressiveness, stability, and functional ability. The sensitive dog must be handled with greater care and quietness in training than the less sensitive animal. Agressive dogs must be trained with firmness; an animal which possesses a structural fault which makes certain of the physical aspects of training a painful experience

Standing to be groomed is a lesson that must be learned at an early age, for the Collie puppy will grow to a huge dog and will be a lot harder to handle if he isn't properly trained to stand for grooming when he is young.

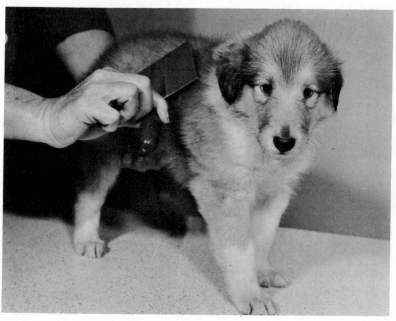

If you cannot take your Collie puppy out for his toilet, train him to newspaper. Paper which has been slightly soiled with his own urine seems to be the most successful training device.

When he finally learns what the paper is for, encourage him by patting him and rewarding him with a favorite piece of dog treat.

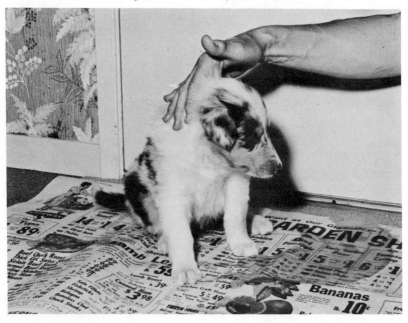

cannot be expected to perform these acts with enjoyment and consistency.

In referring to intelligence we mean, of course, canine intelligence. Dogs are supposedly unable to reason, since that portion of the brain which, in humans, is the seat of the reasoning power is not highly developed in the dog. Yet there have been so many reported incidents of canine behavior that seemingly could not have been actuated by instinct, training, stored knowledge, or the survival factor, that we are led to wonder if the dog may not possess some primitive capacity for reasoning which, in essence, is so different from the process of human reasoning that it has been overlooked, or is as yet beyond the scope of human comprehension.

Training begins the instant the puppies in the nest feel the touch of your hand and are able to hear the sound of your voice. Once the pup is old enough to run and play, handle him frequently, petting him, making a fuss over him, speaking in soothing and pleasant tones and repeating his name over and over again. When you bring him his meals, call him by name and coax him to "come." As time passes, he associates the command "Come!" with a pleasurable experience and will come immediately upon command. Every time he obeys a command he should be praised or rewarded. When calling your puppies to their food, it is good practice to use some kind of distinguishing sound accompanying the command—a clucking or "beep" sound. It is amazing how this distinctive sound will be retained by the dog's memory, so that years after it has ceased to be used he will still remember and respond to the sound.

Some professional trainers and handlers put soft collars on tiny pups with a few inches of thin rope attached to the collar clip. The puppies, in play, tug upon these dangling pieces of rope hanging from the collars of their litter mates, thus preparing the youngsters for easy leash breaking in the future. In training the pup to the leash, be sure to use a long leash and coax, do not drag, the reluctant puppy, keeping him always on your left side. Never use the leash as an implement of punishment.

Housebreaking is usually the tragedy of the novice dog owner. We who have Collies are fortunate in this respect since, as a breed, they are basically clean and easily housebroken. Many Collies which are raised outside in a run never need to be actually housebroken, preferring to use the ground for their act and seemingly sensing the fact that the house is not to be soiled. Dogs tend to defecate in areas

Training your Collie to come upon command is simple if he is properly trained to walk on a lead. This Collie is nearly being dragged to his mistress' feet while she is repeating the command "COME" over and over again.

which they, or other dogs, have previously soiled, and will go to these spots if given the chance. Directly after eating or waking, a puppy almost inevitably has to relieve himself. If he is in the house and makes a mistake, it is generally your fault, as you should have recognized these facts and removed him in time to avert disaster. If, after you have taken him out, he comes in and soils the floor or rug, he must be made to realize that he has done wrong. Scold him with, "Shame! Shame!" and rush him outside. Praise him extravagantly when he has taken advantage of the great outdoors. Sometimes if you catch him preparing to void in the house, a quick, sharp "No" will stop the proceedings and allow you time to usher him out. Never rub his nose in his excretia. Never indulge in the common practice of striking the puppy with a rolled up newspaper or with your hand. If you do, you may be training your dog either to be hand shy, to be shy of paper or to bite the newsboy. Your hand should be used only in such a way that your dog recognizes it as that part of you which implements your voice, to pet and give pleasure. In house-breaking, a "No" or "Shame" appropriately used and delivered in an admonishing tone is punishment enough.

A dog which will attain the size of a Collie is seldom broken to paper in the house. If your dog has been so trained and subsequently you wish to train him to use the outdoors, a simple way to teach him this is to move to the outside the paper he has used, anchoring it with stones. Lead the dog to the paper when you know he is ready to void. Each day make the paper smaller until it has completely disappeared and the pup will have formed the habit of going on the spot previously occupied by the paper. Puppies tend to prefer to void on a surface similar in texture to that which they used in their first few weeks of life. Thus a pup who has had access to an outside run is easily housebroken, preferring the feel of ground under him. Smaller breeds are sometimes raised on wire-bottom pens to keep them free of intestinal parasites. Occasionally puppies so raised have been brought into homes with central heating that employs an open grate-covered duct in the floor. To the pup the grate feels similar to his former wire-bottomed pen. The result, as you can well imagine, gives rise to much profanity and such diligence that the youngster is either rapidly housebroken or just as rapidly banished to live outdoors.

Once the Collie has learned to come upon command, he should be rewarded with a few pats and some of the 'sweet talk' that Collies seem to love and enjoy.

If your Collie has the annoying habit of jumping up on you, or anyone else, just raise your knee as he jumps and it will knock him off balance. A few times of the 'knee treatment' and he will quickly be broken of this terrible habit. Imagine how a small child would feel if a large, strange Collie jumped up to lick her face?

One of the fundamental steps in training a Collie is that he walks properly on a lead and stays at your heel as you walk along with him. The normal Collie walk is much faster than a human walk, thus the Collie must retard his natural gait to be in step with you.

If your Collie is to be a housedog, a lot of grief can be avoided by remembering a few simple rules. Until he is thoroughly clean in the house, confine him to one room at night, preferably a tile or linoleum-floored room that can be cleaned easily. Tie him so that he cannot get beyond the radius of his bed or confine him to a dog house within the room; few dogs will soil their beds or sleeping quarters. Feed at regular hours and you will soon learn the interval between the meal and its natural result and take the pup out in time. Give water only after meals until he is housebroken. Puppies, like inveterate drunks, will drink constantly if the means are available, and there is no other place for surplus water to go but out. The result is odd puddles at odd times.

"No," "Shame," "Come," and "Good boy" (or "girl"), spoken in an appropriate tone, are the basic communications you will use in initial training.

If your pup is running free and he doesn't heed your command to come, do not chase him—he will only run away or dodge your attempts to catch him and your control over him will be completely lost. Attract his attention by calling his name and, when he looks in your direction, turn and run away from him, calling him as you do so. In most instances he will quickly run after you. Even if it takes a great deal of time and much exasperation to get him to come to you, never scold him once he has. Praise him instead. *A puppy should only be scolded when he is caught in the act of doing something he shouldn't do.* If he is scolded even a few minutes after he has committed his error, he will not associate the punishment with the crime and will be bewildered and unhappy about the whole thing, losing his trust in you.

Puppies are inveterate thieves. It is natural for them to steal food from the table. The "No!" and "Shame!" command, or reprimand,

Every Collie puppy should have a bed of his own. When he misbehaves, he should be scolded and placed into his bed and ordered to stay there.

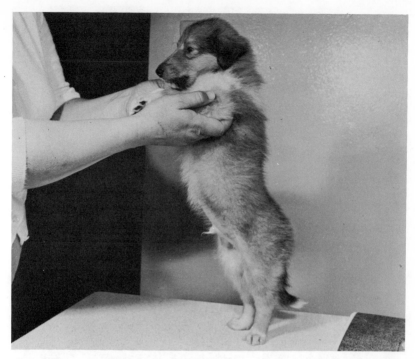

Your Collie puppy should be handled frequently so he will be accustomed to being handled when he is large enough to emphasize his displeasure. Examine your puppy for parasites and hair knots regularly. It trains him in allowing himself to be handled at the same time.

should be used to correct this breach of manners. The same commands are employed when the pup uses your living room couch as a sleeping place. Many times dogs are aware that they must not sleep on the furniture but are clever enough to avoid punishment by using the sofa only when you are out. They will hastily leave the soft comfort of the couch when they hear you approaching and greet you in wide-eyed innocence, models of canine virtue. Only the tell-tale hairs, the dent in the cushion, and the body heat on the fabric are clues to the culprit's dishonesty. This recalls the tale of the dog who went just a step further. So clever was he that when his master approached, he would leap from the couch and, standing before it, blow upon the cushions to dislodge the loose hairs and cool the cushion's surface. The hero of this tale of canine duplicity was not identified as to breed, but we are sure that such intelligence could only have been displayed by a Collie.

Whatever you do, don't feed your dog while you are eating and discourage the family from offering table scraps at any time. Imagine a fully grown Collie jumping on a dinner guest begging for food?

If, like the dog in the story, the pup persists in committing this misdemeanor, we must resort to another method to cure him. Where before we used a positive approach, we must now employ a negative and rather sneaky method. The idea is to trick the pup into thinking that when he commits these crimes he punishes himself and that we have been attempting to stop him from bringing this punishment down upon his head. To accomplish this end with the unregenerate food thief, tie a tempting morsel of food to a long piece of string. To the string attach several empty tin cans or small bells, eight to ten inches apart. Set the whole contraption on the kitchen or dining-room table, with the food morsel perched temptingly on an accessible edge. Leave the room and allow the little thief to commit his act of dishonesty. When you hear the resultant racket, rush into the room, sternly mouthing the appropriate words of reproach. You will generally find a thoroughly chastened pup who, after one or two such lessons, will eye any tabled food askance and leave it strictly alone.

The use of mousetraps is a neat little trick to cure the persistent sofa-hopper. Place two or three set traps on the couch area the dog prefers and cover them with a sheet of newspaper. When he jumps up on the sofa, he will spring the traps and leave that vicinity in a great and startled hurry.

These methods, or slight variations, can be used in teaching your pup to resist many youthful temptations such as dragging and biting rugs, furniture, tablecloths, draperies, curtains, etc.

The same approach, in essence, is useful in teaching the pup not to jump up on you or your friends and neighbors. You can lose innumerable friends if your mud-footed dog playfully jumps up on the visitor wearing a new suit or dress. If the "No!" command alone does not break him of this habit, hold his front legs and feet tightly in your hands when he jumps up and retain your hold. The pup finds himself in an uncomfortable and unnatural position standing on his hind legs alone. He will soon tug and pull to release his front legs from your hold. Retain your hold in the face of his struggles until he is heartily sick of the strained position he is in. A few such lessons and he will refrain from committing an act which brings such discomfort in its wake.

Remember that only by positive training methods can you gain the control which is the basis of successful training and these tricky methods do not give you that control. They are simply short-cut ways of quickly rectifying nuisance habits but do nothing to establish the "rapport" which must exist between trainer and dog.

Teach your Collie always to be friendly with other people. The protective instinct is strongly inherent in our breed and specific training to develop it is not generally needed.

During the entire puppy period the basis is being laid for other and more advanced training. The acts of discipline, of everyday handling, grooming, and feeding, are preparation for the time when he is old enough to be taught the meaning of the Sit, Down, Heel, Stand, and Stay commands, which are the first steps in obedience training and

Training your Collie to stay in one place without leaving it, even if you walk away, is a very important part of his training, and one of the tests given to a dog by the kennel club during his obedience tests.

Teaching your Collie to lie down upon command, whether you use hand signals, voice, or both, is important, and one of the simplest lessons for your Collie to learn.

commands which every dog should be taught to obey immediately. Once you have learned how to train your dog and have established complete control, further training is limited only by your own ability and by the natural boundaries which exist within the animal himself.

Don't rush your training. Be patient with small progress. Training for both you and your dog will become easier as you progress. Make sure that whatever you teach him is well and thoroughly learned, and it will never be forgotten. Remember that your dog's inherited character and intelligence form certain limiting patterns.

A Collie can follow an immediate and hot trail if he has been trained to do so, but a cold and complicated trail is beyond his olfactory powers. If we wish to hunt quail or pheasant, we use setters or pointers of whichever of the gun dog breeds we fancy, but we do not use a Collie, simply because gun dogs have been bred specifically for this work and to attempt to train a Collie to equal the gun dog's ability in

Part of the lesson in training your dog to walk properly is to have your Collie stop when you stop. Give your Collie this training where there are few distractions.

the field would be ridiculous and without purpose. For true trailing ability, the bloodhound is the breed supreme. Tracking, as a part of obedience work, is interesting and aids in developing our dog's mental powers, as do the various other obedience tests. Only those who have had no other experience in true trailing would exaggerate our breed's ability in this field to the point of supremacy. Our breed is fit and capable of doing many things and doing them well. The Collie's service to mankind is so wide and varied that we have a multitude of outlets for his true abilities. Let us then stress the Collie's undeniable worth and inherited ability to perform in these various fields, rather than in some activity in which his capabilities are limited by breed pattern.

But to return to fundamental training, let us review the few and basic truths set forth in this chapter. Remember to use simple common sense when you approach the task of training. Approach it with ease and confidence. Control yourself if you wish to control your dog, for control is the vital element in all training. Realize the limitations as well as the abilities of your dog, and the final product of your training zeal will bring you pride in accomplishment, pride in yourself and your ability, and pride in your Collie.

This Collie is being judged during Advanced Obedience Trials and he is performing a broad jump in perfect style. His mistress has every right to be proud of him.

10.

Training for the Show Ring

So many things of beauty or near perfection are so often marred and flawed by an improper approach to their finish. A Renoir or an El Greco tacked frameless to a bathroom wall is no less a thing of art, yet loses importance by its limited environment and presentation. Living things, too, need this finish and preparation to exhibit their worth to full advantage. The beauty of a flower goes unrecognized if withered petals and leaves mar its perfection and the living wonder of a fine dog is realized only in those moments when he stands or moves in quiet and balanced beauty. The show ring is a ready frame in which to display your dog. The manner in which he is presented within that frame is up to you.

If you contemplate showing your Collie, as so many of you who read this book do, it is of the utmost importance that your dog be as well and fully trained for exhibition as he is for general gentlemanly conduct in the home. Insufficient or improper training or faulty handling can result in lower show placings than your dog deserves and can quite conceivably ruin an otherwise promising show career. In the wider sense, and of even more importance to the breed as a whole, is the impression your Collie in the show ring projects to the gallery. Every Collie shown becomes a representative of the breed in the eyes of the onlookers, so that each dog becomes a symbol of all Collie dogs when he is on exhibition. Inside the ring ropes your dog will be evaluated by the judges as an individual; beyond the ropes, a breed will be judged by the behavior of your dog.

When you enter your Collie in a show, you do so because you believe that he or she is a good enough specimen of the breed to afford competition to, and perhaps win over, the other dogs entered. If your dog is as good as you think he is, he certainly deserves to be shown to full advantage if you expect him to win or place in this highly competitive sport. A novice handler with a quality Collie

Roy Ayers, Jr. started his showmanship career with the same dog his sister started with before Roy was born. The Collie, Ch. Conrad's Sweet Expression, had been retired from the show ring for five years, but for sentimental reasons he was brought out of retirement so that Roy could show him. Roy won this time (Junior Showmanship Class) and the Collie won Best of Breed . . . at nine years old!

which is untrained, unruly, or phlegmatic, cannot give competition to a dog of equal, or even lesser, merit which is well trained and handled to full advantage.

Novice owners frequently bring untrained dogs to shows so that they can become accustomed to the strange proceedings and surroundings, hopefully thinking that, in time, the dog himself will learn to behave in the wanted manner. Often the novice's training for the show ring begins in desperate and intense endeavor within the show ring itself. Confusion for both dog and handler can be the only result of such a program. Preparation for showing by both dog and handler must begin long in advance of actual show competition.

Let us assume that you have been fortunate enough to breed or purchase a puppy who appears to possess all the necessary qualifications for a successful show career. Training for that career should begin from the moment you bring him home, or if you are the breeder, from the time he is weaned. This early training essentially follows the same pattern as does fundamental training in conduct. Again you begin by establishing between yourself and the puppy the happy relationship which, in time, becomes the control so necessary to all training. Handle the puppy frequently, brush him, examine his teeth, set him up in a show stance, and stroke his back slowly. Move him on a loose leash, talking to him constantly in a happy, friendly tone. Make all your movements in a deliberate and quiet manner. Praise and pat the puppy often, thus establishing an easy and happy rapport during this period. This is simple early preparation for the more exact training to come.

It's a simple step from the backyard to the show ring. All of your training has been for the moment you and your Collie step before the judge.

During this period the owner and prospective handler should take the opportunity to refresh or broaden his own knowledge. Reread the standard, and with this word picture in mind, build a mental reproduction of the perfect Collie: his structure, balance, gait, and movement. Critically observe the better Collie handlers at shows to see how they set and gait their dogs. Only by accumulating insight and knowledge such as this can you succeed in the training which will bring out the best features of your own future show dog.

Let us assume that your puppy is now old enough to show, or that you have acquired a young dog for whom you plan a show career. Beginning long before the show in which you are going to start him (several weeks at least), you introduce him to the "tidbit." This can be any bit of food which the dog relishes immensely and which is entirely different from the kind of food used in his regular diet.

When your Collie performs perfectly for you, reward him with some of his favorite treats, but don't overdo this "treat rewarding" business or your Collie will be performing all day and expect rewards every time he does it.

Sandamac's Mr. Shane was a fine example of a well trained dog. He had his C.D. when he was a year old puppy and before he was 1½ years old he had his C.D.X.

The tidbit, then, is a tasty piece of food which the dog likes and which is not given to him at any other time. Boiled liver, in chunks, is most generally used, but dogs can be shown with liverwurst, peanuts, turkey, or various other treats which the individual animal might particularly relish. If you choose liver as your tidbit, brown it in the oven for a few minutes after you have boiled it. This tends to remove the greasiness from the surface and keeps it from crumbling excessively, making it much easier to handle and carry in your pocket in the show ring.

Some dogs are alerted in the show ring by the use of a particular toy, such as a rubber mouse that squeaks when pressed.

It is a great thrill to receive the nod from the judges that YOU WON! It is only patience and fortitude that makes a winner.

We will assume that you now have your dog trained to stand easily and naturally on a loose leash for a reasonable period of time. The next stop in show training is to teach your dog to move properly when on leash. Keeping the dog on your left side, move him forward at a slow trot, checking him sharply when he tends to pull out or break stride. The leash should be kept loose. When you come to the end of the allotted run and turn to start back, do not jerk the dog around; instead give him more leash freedom and allow him to come around easily without a change of leads, meanwhile speaking to him quietly. When he has completed the turn, draw him to you with the leash and continue moving back to the starting point. At the finish pat and praise him.

While you are teaching your dog the elements of ring deportment, take stock of the pupil himself. To do this correctly you will need assistance. Have someone else put the dog through his paces, handling him as you have and as he will be handled in the show ring.

Observe the dog carefully to determine when he looks his best. Should he be stretched out a bit when posing? Does he have better balance and outline if his hind legs are not pulled too far back? At what rate of speed, when moving, does he perform his best?

Pretend that you are a judge. Envision the perfect Collie, and employing your knowledge of the standard as a yardstick, study your dog as though he were a strange animal. From this study you will see many things, tiny nuances, that will aid you in showing your dog to the best possible advantage in open competition.

Once he has mastered the show training you have given him, you must take every opportunity to allow strangers and friends to go over your dog, much in the manner of a judge, while you pose and gait him, so that he will become used to a judge's unaccustomed liberties. It would be well to enter your Collie in a few outdoor sanction matches now, to acquaint him with the actual conditions under which he will be shown. During all this time, of course, the character and temperament of your dog, as well as his physical assets, must be taken into consideration as it must in all types of training and the most made of the best he has.

This outdoor Collie show may bring your Collie into contact with other dogs for the first time. Don't keep your Collie so isolated that he has no canine friends or he won't act properly at shows where there may be scores of other dogs.

Often a handler showing a dog which has not had sufficient training must use other methods to get the most from the animal. We must remember, too, that unless specifically trained to one particular method, a dog may be presented to better advantage when handled in an entirely different manner. It is necessary to attract the attention of some dogs by strange noises, either oral or mechanical. You will also often see handlers squat down on the right side of their animal and set the dog's legs and feet in the desired position. But a dog set up by hand in this manner generally lacks the grace and flow of lines that the naturally posed dog shows to such good advantage.

There is, of course, that paragon of all show dogs, that canine jewel and handler's delight—the alert, curious animal who takes a

Sara Barbaresi, famous author of "How to Raise and Train a Collie" has just won Best in Puppy Class with Starberry Royal Ballet at the 1961 Collie Club of America Show. The judge is Billy Aschenbrenner.

Ch. Collinette Crusade, bred by R. E. Collins, was shipped to Japan to improve the Collie breed there.

keen interest in the world around him and stands in proud and easy naturalness at the end of his long leash, head and ears up, posing ever minute he is in the ring. But remember, even this super-show dog has had some training in ring manners.

In some instances the dog's master stands outside of the ring in full view of his animal while someone else handles him in the ring. The dog will watch his master, keeping his head and ears up and wearing an alert expression. This is called "double-handling" and is sometimes frowned upon by other members of the showing fraternity.

It is of the utmost importance that you never become blind to your dog's faults, but at the same time realize his good features and attempt to exploit these when in the ring. If your dog is a year old or older, do not feed him the day before the show. This will make him more eager for the tidbit when in the ring. Make sure your dog is in good physical shape, in good coat, clean and well groomed. If a bath is necessary, give it to him several days before the show so the natural oils will have time to smooth the coat and give it a natural sheen. Be sure he is not thirsty when he enters the ring and that he has emp-

In nearly every show the handler of the Collie is marked with a number which is used to identify both her and the Collie.

At an Open Bench Show, this portable run is ideal, but part of it should be closed in with a bit of canvas so your Collie can have some protection from the wind and sun.

tied himself before showing, or his movement will be cramped and he will act uncomfortable.

School yourself to be at ease in the ring when handling your dog, for if you are tense and nervous, it will communicate itself to the dog and he will display the same emotional stress. In the ring, keep one eye on your dog and the other on the judge. One never knows when a judge might turn from the animal he is examining, look at your dog, and perhaps catch him in an awkward moment.

Your Collie requires no trimming or primping to make him ready to show as do the representatives of so many other breeds. He is to be shown as nature made him, without any artificial means of beautification. If his nails need clipping, tend to it at least four days before show time so that if you should cut too deeply, the nail will have time to heal.

On the morning of the show, leave your home early enough so that you will have plenty of time to be benched and tend to any last minute details which may come up. When the class before yours is in the ring, give your dog a last quick brush, then run a towel over his coat to bring out the gloss. Should his coat be dull, a few drops of brilliantine, rubbed between the palms of your hands and then sparingly applied to the dog's coat, will aid in eliminating the dullness. Some handlers wipe a slightly dampened towel over the coat just before entering the ring to achieve the same effect. White grooming chalk or cornstarch, applied to the white areas of the coat and then brushed out, helps make these sections appear whiter and cleaner.

Bring to the show with you: a water pail, towel, brush, comb, suppositories in a small jar, white grooming chalk, a bench chain, a chain choke collar, and a light six-foot leash for showing. If the dog has not emptied himself, insert a suppository in his rectum when you take him to the exercising ring. If you forget to bring the suppositories, use instead two paper matches, wet with saliva, from which you have removed the sulphur tips.

In the ring, the handler constantly endeavors to minimize his charge's faults while attempting to inveigle the judge into seeing his virtues. There are several little tricks which the knowing handler employs to accomplish his ends. Should the dog stand east and west in front, the legs must be set correctly by hand. Grasp the dog by the elbow, not the forearm, and gently turn the elbow outward and away from the body until the feet rest parallel to each other. A dog showing lack of rear angulation is offered the tidbit from in front with a pushing motion, while the handler crowds closer to the animal than usual. This causes the dog to sink slightly in the rear quarters, giving the illusion of greater angulation than is actually present. It is good practice, with a dog of high vigor, to have someone who is not showing take him for a good long run before your class comes up. This will take the edge off his exuberance so he will handle with greater steadiness in the ring, and will not bring the handler into the ring in an exhausted condition.

Following is a chart listing the dog-show classes and indicating eligibility in each class, with appropriate remarks. This chart will tell you at a glance which is the best class for your dog.

DOG-SHOW CLASS CHART

CLASS	ELIGIBLE DOGS	REMARKS
PUPPY—6 months and under 9 months	All puppies from 6 months up to 9 months.	
PUPPY—9 months and under 12 months	All puppies from 9 months to 12 months.	
NOVICE	Any dog or puppy which has not won an adult class (over 12 months), or any higher award, at a point show.	After one first-place Novice win, cannot be shown again in the class.
BRED BY EXHIBITOR	Any dog or puppy, other than a Champion, which is owned and bred by exhibitor.	Must be shown only by a member of immediate family of breeder-exhibitor, *i.e.*, husband, wife, father, mother, son, daughter, brother, sister.
AMERICAN-BRED	All dogs or puppies whelped in the U.S. or possessions, except Champions.	
OPEN DOGS	All dogs, 6 months of age or over, including Champions and foreign-breds.	Canadian and foreign champions are shown in open until acquisition of American title. By common courtesy, most American Champions are entered only in Specials.
SPECIALS CLASS	American Champions.	Compete for B.O.B., for which no points are given.

Each sex is judged separately. The winners of each class compete against each other for Winners and Reserve Winners. The animal designated as Winner is awarded the points. Reserve Winners receive no points. Reserve Winners can be the second dog in the class from which the Winners Dog was chosen. The Winners Male and Winners Female (Winners Dog and Winners Bitch) compete for Best of Winners. The one chosen Best of Winners competes against the Specials for Best of Breed, and the Best of Breed winner goes into the Working Dog Group. If the dog is fortunate enough to top this group, his final step is to compete against the other group winners for the Best in Show title.

When Best of Breed is awarded, Best of Opposite Sex is also chosen. A Collie which has taken the points in its own sex as Winners, yet has been defeated for Best of Winners, can still be awarded Best of Opposite Sex if there are no animals of its sex appearing in the ring for the Best of Breed award.

Champions are made by the point system. Only the Winners Dog and Winners Bitch receive points, and the amount of points won depends upon the number of Collies of its own sex the dog has defeated in the classes (not by the number entered). The United

It is cruel to leave your Collie in an exposed run where he cannot have shade from the strong sun. Never leave your dog alone as there are plenty of dog-nappers looking for championship-quality Collies.

States is divided into five regional point groups by the A.K.C., and the point rating varies with the region in which the show is held. Consult a show catalogue for regional rating. A dog going Best of Winners is allowed the same number of points as the animal of the opposite sex which it defeats if the points are of a greater amount than it won by defeating members of its own sex. No points are awarded for Best of Breed.

To become a Champion, a dog must win fifteen points under a minimum of three different judges. In accumulating these points, the dog must win points in at least two major (three points or more) shows, under different judges. Five points is the maximum amount that can be won at any given show. If your dog wins a group, he is entitled to the highest number of points won in any of the working breeds by the dogs he defeats in the group if the points exceed the amount he has won in his own breed. If the show is a Collie Specialty, then the Best of Breed winner automatically becomes the Best in Show dog. No points are awarded at Match or Sanctioned shows.

Remember that showing dogs is a sport, not a matter of life and death, so take your lickings with the same smile that you take your winnings, even if it hurts (and it does). Tomorrow is another day, another show, another judge. The path of the show dog is never strewn with roses, though it may look that way to the novice handler who seems, inevitably, to step on thorns. Always be a good sport don't run the other fellow's dog down because he has beaten yours, and when a Collie goes into the group, give him your hearty applause even if you don't like the dog, his handler, his owner, and his breeding. Remember only that he is a Collie, a representative of your breed and therefore the best darn dog in the group.

We hope that this chapter will help the novice show handler to find greater ease and certainty in training for show and handling in the ring and thus experience more pleasure from exhibiting. Competition is the spice of life, and a good Collie should be shown to his best advantage, for his own glory and for the greater benefit of our wonderful breed.

II.
Shows and Judging

The basic reason for the dog show and the object in the gathering together of representative animals of the breed in open competition seem to have been mislaid in the headlong pursuit for ribbons, trophies, and points. These prizes undoubtedly lead to kennel-name popularity, which in turn produces greater and more profitable puppy sales and stud services, but they are not the end in themselves. They are given simply as tokens of achievement in a much larger pattern which has no direct relation to economy. The graded selection of various dogs according to individual quality by a competent, unbiased judge enables earnest breeders to weigh and evaluate the products of certain breedings and strains. It helps them to evaluate their own breeding procedures in relation to comparative quality, and to give them an idea as to which individuals or breeding lines can act as correctives to the faults inherent in their own breeding. Here the yardstick of the official standard is used to measure the defects or virtues of individual animals and of the breed as a whole for the edification and tabulation of both the knowing breeder and the novice. This is what a dog show should mean to the exhibitor. But with the quality of judging so often displayed, it is no wonder that the showing of dogs has degenerated into a rat race for ribbons, points, and tarnished glory.

Essentially the judge should be an intermediary between the present and the future because his decisions shape the trends for better or for worse. If these trends lead to undesirable results, there will be deterioration instead of an ever-closer approach to the breed ideal. The judge is a sounding board, a calculator of degrees of excellence, an instrument for computing worth. He can, with each assignment, give something of enduring value toward breed improvement. As such, he must not only be entirely familiar with the Collie standard, but must also understand every element of structure and balance. And almost more important, the judge must be able to

175

Coronation Flame, owned by Isabel Chamberlin.

see and evaluate each of those tiny nuances of quality which can establish the superiority of one animal over another of apparently equal excellence.

Judges should confine themselves to judging only those breeds with which they have had personal experience. A thorough reading of the standard and the appearance as an apprentice judge three times do not make anyone an authority on the breed. There should certainly be a more exacting test of ability before a person is granted a license to judge. We are all conscious of the fact that there are some people who could be in a breed all their lives, read every book published about the breed, and still not qualify as competent judges, simply because they do not possess that special gift that brings clarity and sureness to decision. By the same token, there are perhaps others who do not judge who have that "feel" for a good dog, that gift to select surely, which, when combined with knowledge and integrity, makes the completely competent judge.

In the interest of clarity and simplicity as well as for the edification of the ringsider, a definite pattern of procedure should be adhered to by the Collie judge. All entries in any particular class should be lined up in catalogue order opposite the judge's table. The judge should step into the center of the ring and signal the handlers to circle the ring once or twice, with the dogs maintaining an easy trot. The class should then be halted and the dogs left at rest as the judge calls each dog separately to the center of the ring for individual examination. The judge should approach the dog from the front and, speaking kindly to him, begin his close examination. Unnecessary handling by the judge is poor practice. There is no reason, other than unsureness by the judge, for bouncing the animal's back like a mattress inspector, pulling the tail up or down, poking here and there as though frisking the dog for dangerous weapons, or any of the other ridiculous actions sometimes indulged in by judges.

After the individual animal has been examined in the center of the ring, the judge should ask to have him gaited at a slow trot, toward and away from him, to evaluate movement coming and going. Following this, the dog should be gaited around the ring at a slow trot, to establish his quality in profile movement. When all the animals in the class have been individually examined as described, the entire class should be requested to walk around the ring several times and then to proceed at a slow trot until the judge has decided upon his placements.

Bonnydale Nightshade, owned by Julia Finnegan.

The judge should not only pick his first four dogs, but place the others in the class in the order of their excellence as he sees them. He should know, and, indeed, announce to the handlers of each of the first four dogs placed, the reasons for his selections. Should the judge be unable to explain his placings clearly and concisely, he should refrain from further Collie judging. If this procedure would become an A.K.C. rule, there would undoubtedly be several judges now officiating who would hesitate to accept future assignments. It should also be made mandatory, for the same reasons as mentioned above, for a judge to submit to the A.K.C. a written criticism of all dogs placed by him at any given show.

Ch. Starberry Solace, owned by writer Sara Barbaresi.

Ch. Windcall's Tar 'n Feathers. Photo by Evelyn M. Shafer.

During the individual examination in the center of the ring, the judge can make mental notes covering each of the dogs brought before him for future reference. The procedure as outlined above can, of course, be varied to individual taste, but basically it is a standard and sound way of judging.

Though there are times when the judge is at fault, we must not forget that there are many times when the exhibitor's evaluation of the judge's placings is faulty. Too many exhibitors know too little about their own breed and are not competent to indulge in criticism. The very structure of dog-show procedure lends itself to dissatisfaction with the judge's decisions. The fact that there can be only three or fewer really satisfied winners in any breed judging, Winner's Male, Winner's Bitch, and Best of Breed, and that they are chosen by one individual who may or may not be competent, leaves

Ch. Alphington Sociable, owned by Mrs. A. E. Newbury. Photo by C. M. Cooke.

a wide range of just or unjust recrimination for the exhibitor to air. Some of the post-mortem denunciation can be attributed directly to the psychological effect of the shows upon the exhibitors themselves.

Almost everyone, at some time or another, has had the urge to engage in some kind of competitive sport. Most exhibitors have arrived at that time of life when most competitive endeavor is too strenuous to be indulged in. Some have been frustrated non-athletes all their lives due to lack of muscular or physical prowess, or because sustained exertion did not fit their behavior patterns. Nevertheless, the fierce flame of competitiveness burns in them, and the dog-show ring provides a wonderful outlet to satisfy this need of expression. Some, without realizing it, find that the show ring provides an outlet for their normal desire to be important, if even for just a few fleeting moments, and it gives others an opportunity to be on the stage before an audience. The greater number of exhibitors are simply proud of their dogs and want to show them and have them evaluated in competition. Since there is no definite scoring for endeavor, merely a personal evaluation of their animals by an individual who can be right or wrong, tension is built and personalities clash.

The exhibitor has put an enormous amount of time, thought, and heartaches in breeding, rearing, and preparation into the show. With most exhibitors, the very fact that they are present signifies they consider their particular dog fine enough to win. All this tends to build up strong feelings which sometimes erupt into strong words.

Undoubtedly the whole procedure is of benefit to the exhibitor. He or she indulges in some measure of physical exercise, finds an outlet for the competitive spirit, and presently soothes built-up

Ch. Conrad's Stop the Music, shown here by the owner Roy Ayers, Sr. A Patterson-Young photo.

emotions by letting off vocal steam. But the end result is not good for the breed, since it results in confusion, especially to the novice who comes to the show to learn.

There will always be with us the chronic griper who must tear down another's dog with unfounded criticism after he has been defeated so that his own animal will appear better than it is. We must also deplore the custom of severe criticism and whispering campaigns against a consistent and deserving winner or stud. This insidious undermining of an animal of worth leads the novice to wonder how any judge had the temerity to put him up, which in turn casts reflections upon the judge's ability and further confounds the tyro who is seeking truth.

Many of the most prominent breeders who have been in the breed for years are judges as well. They are frequently criticized for their show-ring placements because they will put up animals of their own breeding or those of a type similar to the strain they themselves produce. Undeniably, there are many instances in which a dog, handled or owned by an individual who is himself a judge, is given preference, since the breeder-judge officiating at the moment will, in the near future, show under the owner of the dog he has put up and expects the same consideration in return. This is but one of the many ways in which a judge may be influenced, consciously or unconsciously. Regardless of the underlying cause, such practice must be condemned. But in most cases the breeder-judge who elevates animals of his own breeding or dogs of similar type cannot be summarily accused of lack of integrity. The type which he breeds must be the type of Collie he likes and his own interpretation of the standard. It follows, therefore, that this is the type he will put up in all honesty. We may question his taste, knowledge, or interpretation of the standard, but not, in most instances, his ethics or honesty.

It is true that some judges seem to develop special prejudices on particular points of structure and overemphasize some minor fault which they particularly detest. Still, in some instances, this emphasis can be a boon, causing quick elimination of some fault which, if allowed to become concentrated, could become a definite menace to the perfection for which we strive. If judges persist in elevating to the top animals possessing any prevalent fault, the breeders unconsciously follow the trend and produce it, and it becomes incorporated as a dominant within the breed. When such a condition exists, the judges of the breed should be made aware of this tendency

Ch. Limpid of Ladypark, owned by Miss P. M. Grey. Photo by C. M. Cooke.

and, by penalizing it in the ring and vocally stressing this fact in evaluating the animal to its handler, do their share toward its elimination.

We are frequently told that the element of human variance in the interpretation of the standard is responsible for the wide difference of placings from one show to the next. Certainly this is true, but it should be true only to a limited extent. A judge's interpretation of the standard and his knowledge of what is a fault or a credit cannot vary so greatly from show to show if dictated alone by the human equation. Acknowledging the slight variance in placing which the individual judge's interpretation might cause, there is still no excuse for the wide discrepancy and sometimes weird difference in placings, which we see occur too frequently. When we see this type of bad or biased judging, we can only assume that the arbitrator is either dishonest or ignorant and, in either case, is doing the breed great harm.

There are quite a few qualified and earnest judges whose placings should be followed and analyzed, for it is through them that we can evaluate the breeding health of the Collie and know with confidence the individual worth of specific specimens. Judging is not an easy task. It does not generally lead to long and cosy friendships, for once an individual steps into the ring to begin his judiciary assignment, he is no longer an individual but becomes the impartial, wholly objective instrument of the standard. As such, friendship and personal likes or dislikes cannot exist as facets of his make-up. He must judge the dogs before him as they are on that day, without sentiment or favor. This is a task that demands complete subjection of self, high knowledge of the breed, and courage and integrity. It can be easily seen, then, that not too many people could qualify in all these respects and so become completely proficient judges.

The judging situation can be improved. A system should be set up whereby only those who have passed some rigid test would be qualified to judge the breed. Were the ideal condition to exist, we, the breeders and owners, would submit our animals in open competition to the careful scrutiny of a truly competent authority whose integrity was beyond question. We would be able to compare our stock within the ring to see where we had erred. We would be able to measure the worth of breeding theory by the yardstick of a correct interpretation of the standard. We would know then what breeding lines were producing animals closest to the ideal and which individual dogs showed the highest degree of excellence; by thus creating, through the medium of the judge, an authority which we could depend upon, we could establish an easier path to the breed ideal.

12.

The Standard of the Collie

The standard of our breed is precise and all-encompassing without being wordy. If it is read and assimilated it will give the reader as complete as possible a word picture of what a Collie should be. Interpretation might possibly vary slightly, but, to the author's way of thinking, the standard needs no extensive explanation or long discussion. For the novice this would only confuse issues. To the person who knows Collies it is not necessary.

Learn your standard and use it as a yardstick to measure faults and virtues in your stock. Find animals who are superlative in various anatomical sections and so establish in your mind, by comparison, the degrees of excellence as mentioned in the standard. Armed with this knowledge, the eye picture and the word picture, you have a goal for which to strive. Remember that the perfect dog, as depicted by the standard, has never lived and, if he had, the standard would have to be raised, for it must be a star to shoot at, something now beyond reach but perhaps attainable.

COLLIES (ROUGH)

DESCRIPTION AND STANDARD OF POINTS

(Adopted by the Collie Club of America and Approved by The American Kennel Club October 10, 1950)

General Character.—The Collie is a lithe, strong, responsive, active dog, carrying no useless timber, standing naturally straight and firm. The deep, moderately wide chest shows strength, the sloping shoulders and well-bent hocks indicate speed and grace, and the face shows high intelligence. The Collie presents an impressive, proud picture of true balance, each part being in harmonious proportion to every other part and to the whole. Except for the technical description that is essential to this Standard and without which no Standard for the guidance of breeders and judges is ade-

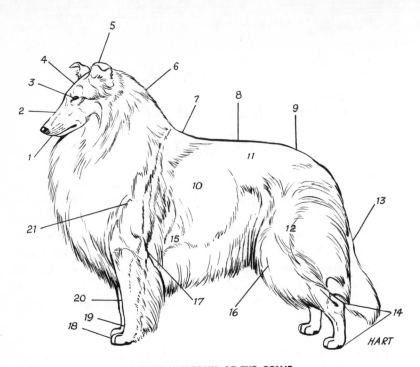

EXTERNAL ANATOMY OF THE COLLIE

1. Muzzle 2. Foreface 3. Eye 4. Skull 5. Ear 6. Neck 7. Withers 8. Back 9. Croup
10. Ribbing 11. Loin 12. Thigh 13. Tail (or Stern) 14. Hock 15. Chest 16. Stifle
17. Elbow 18. Foot 19. Pastern 20. Forearm

quate, it could be stated simply that no part of the Collie ever seems to be out of proportion to any other part. Timidity, frailness, sullenness, viciousness, lack of animation, cumbersome appearance and lack of over-all balance impair the general character.

Head.—The head properties are of great importance. When considered in proportion to the size of the dog, the head is inclined to lightness and never appears massive. A heavy-headed dog lacks the necessary bright, alert, full-of-sense look that contributes so greatly to expression.

Both in front and profile view, the head bears a general resemblance to a well-blunted lean wedge, being smooth and clean in outline and nicely balanced in proportion. On the sides it tapers gradually and smoothly from the ears to the end of the black nose, without being flared out in backskull ("cheeky") or pinched in muzzle ("snipy"). In profile view the top of the backskull and the top of the muzzle lie in two approximately parallel, straight planes of equal length, divided by a very slight but perceptible stop or break.

A mid-point between the inside corners of the eyes (which is the center of a correctly placed stop) is the center of balance in length of head.

The end of the smooth, well-rounded muzzle is blunt but not square. The underjaw is strong, clean-cut and the depth of skull from the brow to the under part of the jaw is not excessive.

The teeth are of good size, meeting in a scissors bite. *Overshot or undershot jaws are undesirable, the latter being more severely penalized.*

There is a very slight prominence of the eyebrows. The backskull is flat, without receding either laterally or backward and the occipital bone is not highly peaked. The proper width of backskull necessarily depends upon the combined length of skull and muzzle and the width of the backskull is less than its length. Thus the

Can. Ch. Sandamac's Sandonna C.D.

correct width varies with the individual and is dependent upon the extent to which it is supported by length of muzzle.

Because of the importance of the head characteristics, *prominent head faults are very severely penalized.*

Eyes.—Because of the combination of the flat skull, the arched eyebrows, the slight stop and the rounded muzzle; the foreface must be chiseled to form a receptacle for the eyes and they are necessarily placed obliquely to give them the required forward outlook. Except for the "Blue Merles," they are required to be matched in color. They are almond-shaped of medium size and never properly appear to be large or prominent. The color is dark and the eye does not show a yellow ring or a sufficiently prominent haw to affect the dog's expression.

The eyes have a clear, bright appearance, expressing intelligent inquisitiveness, particularly when the ears are drawn up and the dog is on the alert.

Int. Ch. Lochinvar of Ladypark, owned by Miss P. M. Grey. Photo by C. M. Cooke.

Ch. Cherry Lady, owned by Mr. R. Adamson. Photo by C. M. Cooke.

In "Blue Merles", dark brown eyes are preferable, but either or both eyes may be merle or china in color without specific penalty.

A large, round, full eye seriously detracts from the desired "sweet" expression. *Eye faults are heavily penalized.*

Ears.—The ears are in proportion to the size of the head and, if they are carried properly and unquestionably "break" naturally, are seldom too small. Large ears usually cannot be lifted correctly off the head and even if lifted they will be out of proportion to the size of the head. When in repose the ears are folded lengthwise and thrown back into the frill. On the alert they are drawn well up on the backskull and are carried about three-quarters erect, with about one-fourth of the ear tipping or "breaking" forward. *A dog with prick ears or low ears cannot show true expression and is penalized accordingly.*

Neck.—The neck is firm, clean, muscular, sinewy and heavily frilled. It is fairly long, carried upright with a slight arch at the

189

nape and imparts a proud, upstanding appearance showing off the frill.

Body.—The body is firm, hard and muscular, a trifle long in proportion to the height. The ribs are well-rounded behind the well-sloped shoulders and the chest is deep, extending to the elbows. The back is strong and level, supported by powerful hips and thighs and the croup is sloped to give a well-rounded finish. The loin is powerful and slightly arched. *Noticeably fat dogs, or dogs in poor flesh, or with skin disease, or with no undercoat are out of condition and are moderately penalized accordingly. In grown males, a monorchid is penalized and a cryptorchid is disqualified.*

Legs.—The fore legs are straight and muscular, with a fair amount of bone considering the size of the dog. A cumbersome appearance is undesirable. *Both narrow and wide placement are penalized.* The

COLLIE FAULTS

The faults of this Collie are: eye too rounded and large, prick ears, roached back, steep short croup, long in loin, long in body, sickle hocks, poor tail carriage (indicating shyness), and too steep in pastern.

COLLIE FAULTS

The faults of this Collie are: Roman nose, ears over-tipped (houndy, not tulip), shows no neck crest, sway-backed, overbuilt behind, no slope of croup, fore assembly pushed too far forward (lacks shoulder angulation), soft in pastern, foot and toe construction poor, lacks rear angulation (stilted) and the tail is too short.

forearm is moderately fleshy and the pasterns are flexible but without weakness. The hind legs are less fleshy, muscular at the thighs, very sinewy, and the hocks and stifles are well bent. *A cowhocked dog or a dog with straight stifles is penalized.* The comparatively small feet are approximately oval in shape. The soles are well padded and tough and the toes are well arched and close together. When the Collie is not in motion, the legs and feet are judged by allowing the dog to come to a natural stop in a standing position so that both the fore legs and the hind legs are placed well apart with the feet extending straight forward. Excessive "posing" is undesirable.

Gait.—The gait or movement is distinctly characteristic of the breed. A sound Collie is not out at the elbows but it does, nevertheless, move toward an observer with its front feet tracking com-

COLLIE FRONTS

1. **Good Front. 2. Too narrow, fiddle-fronted (feet east and west), elbows in. 3. Out at elbows, toes in, will cross front feet when moving.**

paratively close together at the ground. The front legs do not "cross over" nor does the Collie move with a pacing or rolling gait. Viewed from the front, one gains the impression that the dog is capable of changing its direction of travel almost instantaneously, as indeed it is. When viewed from the rear, the hind legs, from the hock joint to the ground, move in comparatively close-together, parallel, vertical planes. The hind legs are powerful and propelling. Viewed from the side, the gait is not choppy but smooth. The reasonably long, "reaching" stride is even, easy, light and seemingly effortless.

Tail.—The tail is moderately long, the bone reaching to the hock joint or below. It is carried low when the dog is quiet, the end having an upward twist or "swirl." When gaited or when the dog is excited, it is carried gaily but not over the back.

Coat.—The well-fitting, proper-textured coat is the crowning glory of the Rough Variety of Collie. It is abundant except on the head and legs. The outer coat is straight and harsh to the touch. *A soft, open outer coat or a curly outer coat, regardless of quantity, is penalized.* The undercoat, however, is soft, furry and so close together that it is difficult to see the skin when the hair is parted. The coat is very abundant on the mane and frill. The face or mask is smooth. The fore legs are smooth and well feathered to the back of the pasterns. The hind legs are smooth below the hock joints. Any feathering below the hocks is removed for the show ring. The hair on the tail is very profuse and on the hips it is long and bushy.

The texture, quantity and the extent to which the coat "fits the dog" are important points.

Color.—The four recognized colors are "Sable and White," "Tri-color," "Blue Merle" and "White." There is no preference among them. The "Sable and White" is predominantly sable (a fawn sable color of varying shades from light gold to dark mahogany) with white markings usually on the chest, neck, legs, feet and the tip of the tail. A blaze may appear on the foreface or back-skull or both. The "Tri-color" is predominantly black, carrying white markings as in a "Sable and White" and has tan shadings on and about the head and legs. The "Blue Merle" is a mottled or "marbled" color, predominantly blue-gray and black with white markings as in the "Sable and White" and usually has tan shadings as in the "Tri-color." The "White" is predominantly white, preferably with sable or tri-color markings. Blue merle coloring is undesirable in "Whites."

Size.—Dogs are from 24 to 26 inches at the shoulder and weigh from 60 to 75 pounds. Bitches are from 22 to 24 inches at the shoulder, weighing from 50 to 65 pounds. *An undersize or an oversize Collie is penalized according to the extent to which the dog appears to be undersize or oversize.*

Expression.—Expression is one of the most important points in considering the relative value of Collies. "Expression" like the

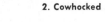

COLLIE REARS

1. Good Rear	2. Cowhocked

term "character" is difficult to define in words. It is not a fixed point as in color, weight or height and it is something the uninitiated can properly understand only by optical illustration. In general, however, it may be said to be the combined product of the shape and balance of the skull and muzzle, the placement, size, shape and color of the eyes and the position, size and carriage of the ears. An expression that shows sullenness or which is suggestive of any other breed is entirely foreign. The Collie cannot be judged properly until its expression has been carefully evaluated.

DISQUALIFICATION

Body.—In grown males, a cryptorchid is disqualified.

COLLIES (SMOOTH)

DESCRIPTION AND STANDARD OF POINTS

(Adopted by the Collie Club of America and Approved by The American Kennel Club October 10, 1950)

The Smooth Variety of Collie is judged by the same Standard as the Rough Variety except that the references to the quantity and the distribution of the coat are not applicable to the Smooth Variety, which has a hard, dense, smooth coat.

Ch. Peterblue Patricia, owned by Miss K. Alexander and Miss E. Dundas Monat. Photo by C. M. Cooke.

13.

Collie Temperament

The first definition of the word "temperament" in Webster's reads: "Internal constitution in respect to balance or mixture of qualities or parts." This is, to say the least, a vague and general definition, and one which can stand considerable explanation and broadening when it is used with reference to the Collie.

The word "temperament," in its general application, embraces character, sensitivity, discrimination, spirit, and intellect. It can denote either the absence or presence of one or more of these psychological traits. As a definitive, the word is therefore too wide in scope to have direct meaning. But we are not as concerned with the word as we are with its broad application. What is the true Collie temperament? How is temperament, good or bad, transmitted? Why does a Collie possess a temperament which can be specifically right or wrong for the breed? What are the essential faults of temperament? Where do these faults come from and can they be corrected? These are the questions that we must have answered if we would understand and be capable of evaluating temperament.

Temperament is not a simple Mendelian trait. It is the sum total of the animal's mental being, his inherited mind structure and his ability to apply it to experience.

Environment, to a limited extent, can influence eventual temperament, particularly as it is applied to early puppy experience. The dog is a creature of habit and imitation, and a shy bitch can cause shy habit patterns in her young by their imitation of her behavior. But influences of environment are acquired characters, not hereditary patterns, and therefore cannot be transmitted as such. The effect of environment on temperament is negligible, since essentially the greater number of breeders and owners supply proper environment for their dogs. The influence of environment, too, is kept within fairly narrow limits by natural and inherited demarcation. If environment did exert a high percentage of influence, how then explain the shy young dog, raised, fed, handled, and housed exactly the same as his mentally normal run-mate?

Let us first come to terms with the full meaning of this thing called temperament. A dog is not just "shy" or "stupid." An animal which displays these traits is mentally unsound, degenerate, or moronic. He is a constant worry to his owner and a danger to himself, his breed, and anyone with whom he comes in contact. Mental degeneration can and will limit the popularity of the breed.

The essence of the Collie as an individual breed is based upon type and temperament. Without type, a dog is not fit to be classified as a Collie. Without temperament, a Collie is not fit to be classified as a dog.

We so often hear the phrase, "He is only slightly shy. I'm taking him to training classes to correct it." If this temperament fault is the rare one of environment, it can, in many cases, be corrected. If it is a slight hereditary mental aberration, it can sometimes be covered up or hidden to all but the canny observer by training. But if the taint of mental instability is present as an inherited factor, it will

Collies usually get along well together, but to be on the safe side, have both dogs on leads when you introduce them. Collies with nasty dispositions should not be bred.

Collies are natural guard dogs . . . and they guard children as well as sheep.

never leave, and to say that a dog is slightly shy is akin to saying a woman is slightly pregnant; there are degrees in both cases, but the fundamental fact cannot be denied and with the passage of time becomes more evident.

Faults of temperament can be divided into the five basic categories which follow. In each instance the faults discussed are the extremes. There are shadings or degrees from the norm to the extreme and, in some instances, an overlapping of temperament defects. We are, of course, using extremes to give a completely clear picture of the faults of temperament, since without complete recognition, correction or elimination is impossible.

A *shy* dog is an oversensitive animal, an introvert whose world is too much for him. He lives in a dark mental shell of his own making, peopled by personal dragons and echoing hollowly to frightful sounds. To this dog, most experience is filled with horror and permeated with fear of the unknown. As a living creature he is a pitiful, craven thing whose constant terror of life pleads for release through peaceful death. This is a dog at the extreme limits of shyness. Sometimes we find a degree of timidity in young dogs or puppies, particularly

Ch. Beulah's Golden Son Fuson, owned by Mrs. N. K. George. Photo by C. M. Cooke.

bitches, which must not be confused with shyness. It is often due to lack of varied experience with strangeness and new activity.

The *sharp-shy* dog is the epitome of bad temperament. He is easily driven to panic by the unfamiliar. When faced with strange surroundings or the approach of one who is not a familiar, the extreme fear-biter will attempt to escape, bites if he thinks he is cornered, urinates, and permeates the premises with a foul odor which emanates from the anal glands. If you own a dog with these defects, you should have it destroyed no matter how painful it is for you to do so. It may be attached to its own household and the inmates and be sweet and kind with the children, but this is only comparable to the counselor's plea for his criminal client who was "good to his mother." This psychologically unstable animal will, if the occasion arises, bite one of its owners in blind panic without even being aware of having done so.

The *dull* dog is so undersensitive to outside stimuli that he lives in an uncaring world of grayness which has no distinctive contrasts. To some people he is a good dog to have around, since he asks for little other than food and shelter. He is quiet in the house and around the grounds, since there is nothing around him of sufficient interest to arouse him to either curiosity or action. He has no individuality and is as much of a companion as an end table. We do not have many individuals of this character (or lack of character) in the breed.

An *overly sharp, or vicious,* dog, unless kept strictly under control or confinement, is as dangerous as a rattlesnake. This is our canine gangster who obeys no law but the ancient one of club and fang. He is an overbearing bully who mistrusts everyone and, like his human counterpart, is a menace to society. He is never to be trusted with strangers or other dogs. This animal is generally undersensitive to bodily discomfort or pain. There are fewer congenitally vicious dogs than shy dogs. An overly aggressive dog can sometimes be made dangerous by environment. He can be trained to attack and bite upon command, and unless he has the intelligence to discriminate,

A good Collie is even willing to share his food with other dogs.

he can become a hair-trigger menace when not under complete control. This same type of animal can be spoiled by over-indulgence and babying until his respect for his owner vanishes, the owner's control is gone, and the dog decides his destiny is his own.

There is also the *distrustful* dog. The animals exhibiting this trait are normal and friendly with their own people, but withdraw hastily when approached by strangers. They do not show fear or other symptoms associated with shyness. They are not inclined to bite, are not barkers or overaggressive. Their attitude is one of negative aloofness to strangers. They can be won over only by close association and even then, the animal itself must be left to make the first actual advances toward friendship.

In the training of working dogs for specific utilitarian purposes, temperament defects are readily detected; but in the breeding of show dogs, or pets, these faults are many times unnoticed or condoned. It is an undeniable truth that we as frequently make excuses for our dog's mental aberrations as we do for our children's.

The true Collie must be an animal fit in body and mentality to do the essential work for which the breed was created. We want a

Collies and Cats get along well together, give them equal affection.

Playing with ropes around Collies can be dangerous as they can tear out a dog's teeth or inadvertently strangle him.

Collie that is sweet, kind, and happy in disposition, yet bold and courageous. He must be alert and eager to please and serve. Above all, he must be highly intelligent, for without intelligence he will not be capable of employing his native temperament and mental ability to the greatest extent. The dog possessing this true Collie temperament has no problems. He has trust and confidence in the world, in its seasons, vagaries, and inhabitants and, therefore, he has trust in himself and is at peace with his environment.

The enduring worth and glory of any breed lies in its service to mankind, but that service cannot be realized unless the animals within the breed possess the necessary mental equipment to fulfill their destiny.

Remember that our Collie is different in temperament and structure from other breeds because he has been made so by biological heredity, and this difference has been accentuated by selective breeding for special functions. This is why correct temperament is so important to the breed. Without it, the very purpose of the breed is destroyed, and without purpose no living thing has worth.

14.
Diseases and First Aid

The dog is heir to many illnesses, and, as with man, it seems that when one dread form has been overcome by some specific medical cure, another quite as lethal takes its place. It is held by some that this cycle will always continue, since it is nature's basic way of controlling population.

There are, of course, several ways to circumvent Dame Nature's lethal plans. The initial step in this direction is to put the health of your dogs in the hands of one who has the knowledge and equipment, mental and physical, to cope competently with your canine health problems. We mean, of course, a modern veterinarian. Behind this man are years of study and experience and a knowledge of all the vast research, past and present, which has developed the remarkable cures and artificial immunities that have so drastically lowered the canine mortality rate as of today.

Put your trust in the qualified veterinarian and "beware of Greeks bearing gifts." Beware, too, of helpful friends who say, "I know what the trouble is and how to cure it. The same thing happened to my dog." Home doctoring by unskilled individuals acting upon the advice of unqualified "experts" has killed more dogs than distemper.

Your Collie is constantly exposed to innumerable diseases through the medium of flying and jumping insects, parasites, bacteria, fungus, and virus. His body develops defenses and immunities against many of these diseases, but there are many more which we must cure or immunize him against if they are not to prove fatal.

We are not qualified to give advice about treatment for the many menaces to your dog's health that exist and, by the same token, you are not qualified to treat your dog for these illnesses with the skill or knowledge necessary for success. We can only give you a resumé of modern findings on the most prevalent diseases and illnesses so that you can, in some instances, eliminate them or the causative agent yourself. Even more important, this chapter will help you recognize their symptoms in time to seek the aid of your veterinarian.

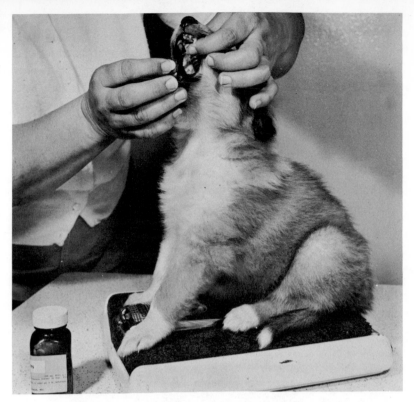

After weighing this healthy Collie pup, the worm pill goes down the throat.

Though your dog can contract disease at any time or any place, he or she is most greatly exposed to danger when in the company of other dogs at dog shows or in a boarding kennel. Watch your dog carefully after it has been hospitalized or sent afield to be bred. Many illnesses have an incubation period, during the early stages of which the animal himself may not show the symptoms of the disease, but can readily contaminate other dogs with whom he comes in contact. It is readily seen, then, that places where many dogs are gathered together, such as those mentioned above, are particularly dangerous to your dog's health.

Parasitic diseases, which we will first investigate, must not be taken too lightly, though they are the easiest of the diseases to cure. Great suffering and even death can come to your dog through these parasites that prey on him if you neglect to realize the importance of both cure and the control of reinfestation.

EXTERNAL PARASITES

The lowly flea is one of the most dangerous insects from which you must protect your dog. It carries and spreads tapeworm, heartworm and bubonic plague, causes loss of coat and weight, spreads skin disease, and brings untold misery to its poor host. These pests are particularly difficult to combat because their eggs—of which they lay thousands—can lie dormant for months, hatching when conditions of moisture and warmth are present. Thus you may think you have rid your dog (and your house) of these devils, only to find that they mysteriously reappear as weather conditions change.

When your dog has fleas, use any good commercial flea powder which contains fresh rotenone. Dust him freely with the powder. It is not necessary to cover the dog completely, since the flea is active and will quickly reach a spot saturated with the powder and die. Rotenone is also fatal to lice. A solution of this drug in pine oil and added to water to be employed as a dip or rinse will kill all insects except ticks. DDT in liquid soap is excellent and long-potent,

Spray your Collie puppy regularly with dog flea and tick repellent. Your petshop can supply you with many different brands.

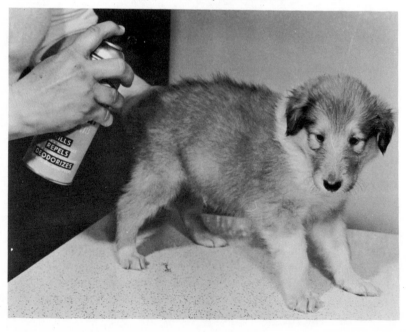

Ch. Inglibrook's Wee Genny, owned by Mr. J. Fendley. Photo by C. M. Cooke.

Ch. Rhodelands Boy, owned by Sr. V. Consiglia. Photo by C. M. Cooke.

its effect lasting for as long as a week. Benzene hexachloride, chlordane, and any number of many new insecticides developed for the control of flies are also lethal to fleas. Whatever specific is prescribed by your veterinarian should also be used on your dog's sleeping quarters as well as on the animal itself. Repeat the treatment in ten days to eliminate fleas which have been newly hatched from dormant eggs.

TICKS

There are many kinds of ticks, all of which go through similar stages in their life process. At some stage in their lives they all find it necessary to feed on blood. Luckily, these insect vampires are fairly easily controlled. The female of the species is much larger than the male, which will generally be found hiding under the female. Care must be taken in the removal of these pests to guard against the mouth parts remaining embedded in the host's skin after the body of the tick is removed. DDT is an effective tick remover. Ether or nail-polish remover touched to the inidvidual tick will cause it to relax

Take your Collie to the veterinarian every six months for a general physical checkup. Remember the old saying: "An ounce of prevention is worth a pound of cure." It's true.

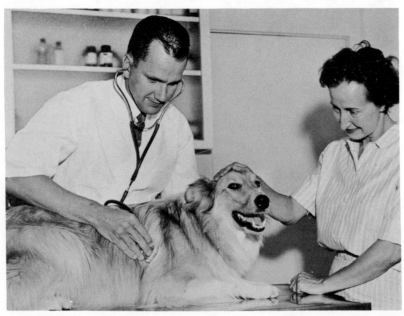

Ch. Ugony's Golden Son of Lad of Riffelsee, owned by Miss D. M. Young.
Photo by C. M. Cooke.

its grip and fall off the host. The heated head of a match from which
the flame has been just extinguished, employed in the same fashion,
will cause individual ticks to release their hold and fall from the
dog. After veterinary tick treatment, no attempt should be made to
remove the pests manually, since the treatment will cause them to
drop by themselves as they succumb.

MITES

There are three basic species of mites that generally infect dogs, the
demodectic mange mite (red mange), the sacroptic mange mite
(white mange), and the ear mite. Demodectic mange is generally
recognized by balding areas on the face, cheeks, and the front parts
of the foreleg, which present a moth-eaten appearance. Reddening
of the skin and great irritation occur as a result of the frantic rubbing
and scratching of affected parts by the animal. Rawness and thicken-

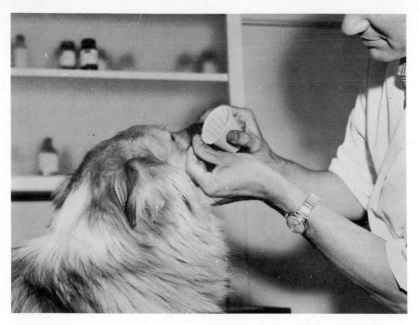

This is the proper way to give your Collie liquids. Pour it into the pocket of the lower jaw.

ing of the skin follows. Not too long ago this was a dread disease in dogs, from which few recovered. It is still a persistent and not easily cured condition unless promptly diagnosed and diligently attended to.

Sarcoptic mange mites can infest you as well as your dog. The resulting disease is known as scabies. This disease very much resembles dry dermatitis, or what is commonly called "dry eczema." The coat falls out and the denuded area becomes inflamed and itches constantly.

Ear mites, of course, infest the dog's ear and can be detected by an accumulation of crumbly dark brown or black wax within the ear. Shaking of the head and frequent scratching at the site of the infestation accompanied by squeals and grunting also are symptomatic of the presence of these pests. Canker of the ear is a condition, rather than a specific disease, which covers a wide range of ear infection and which displays symptoms similar to ear mite infection.

All three of these diseases and ear canker should be treated by your veterinarian. By taking skin scrapings or wax particles from the ear for microscopic examination, he can make an exact diagnosis and recommend specific treatment. The irritations caused by these ailments, unless immediately controlled, can result in loss of appetite and weight and so lower your dog's natural resistance that he is open to the attack of other diseases which his bodily defenses could normally battle successfully.

INTERNAL PARASITES

It seems strange, in the light of new discovery of specific controls for parasitism, that the incidence of parasitic infestation should still be almost as great as it was years ago. This can only be due to lack of realization by the dog owner of the importance of initial prevention and control against reinfestation. Strict hygiene must be adhered to if dogs properly treated are not to be exposed to infestation immediately again. This is particularly true where worms are concerned.

The veterinarian will check your Collie's ears to be sure that they do not need cleaning and that they do not harbor parasites

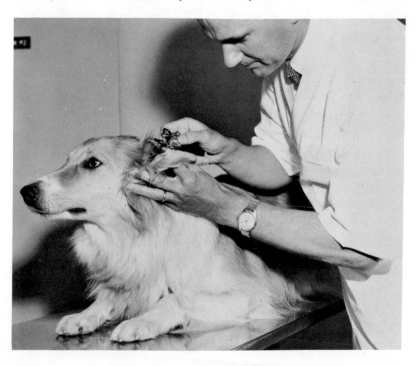

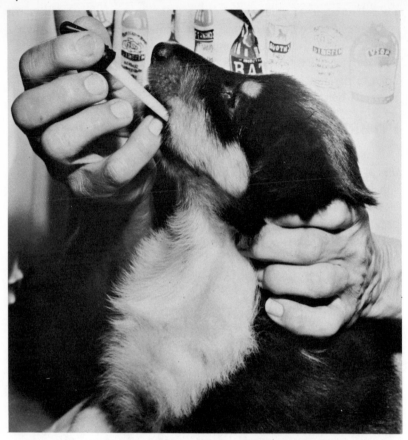

An easy way to give medicine or vitamins is with a plastic eyedropper.

In attempting to rid our dogs of worms, we must not be swayed by amateur opinion. The so-called "symptoms" of worms may be due to many other reasons. We may see the actual culprits in the animal's stool, but even then it is not wise to worm indiscriminately. The safest method to pursue is to take a small sample of your dog's stool to your veterinarian. By a fecal analysis he can advise just what specific types of worms infest your dog and what drugs should be used to eliminate them.

Do not worm your dog because you "think" he should be wormed, or because you are advised to do so by some self-confessed "authority." Drugs employed to expel worms can prove highly dangerous to your dog if used indiscriminately and carelessly, and in many instances the same symptoms that are indicative of the presence of internal parasites can also be the signs of some other affliction.

A word here in regard to that belief that garlic will "cure" worms. Garlic is an excellent flavoring agent, favored by gourmets the world over—but—it will not rid your dog of worms. Its only curative power lies in the fact that, should you use it on a housedog who has worms, the first time he pants in your face you will definitely be cured of ever attempting this pseudo-remedy again.

ROUNDWORM

These are the most common worms found in dogs and can have grave effects upon puppies, which they almost invariably infest. Potbellies, general unthriftiness, diarrhea, coughing, lack of appetite, anemia, are the symptoms. They can also cause verminous pneumonia when in the larvae stage. Fecal examinations of puppy stools

Ch. Debonair of Glenmist, owned by F. Mitchell. Photo by C. M. Cooke.

should be made frequently by your veterinarian if control of these parasites is to be constant. Although theoretically it is possible for small puppies to be naturally worm free, actually most pups are born infested or contract the parasitic eggs at the mother's breast.

The roundworm lives in the intestine and feeds on the dog's partially digested food, growing and laying eggs which are passed out in the dog's stool to be picked up by him in various ways and so cause reinfestation. The life history of all the intestinal worms is a vicious circle, with the dog the beginning and the end host. This worm is yellowish-white in color and is shaped like a common garden worm, pointed at both ends. It is usually curled when found in the stool. There are several different species of this type of worm. Some varieties are more dangerous than others. They discharge toxin within the dog, and the movement of larvae to important internal sections of the dog's body can cause death.

The two drugs most used by kennel owners for the elimination of roundworms are N-butyl-chloride and tetrachlorethylene, but

Ch. Riffelsee Reward of Glenmist, owned by Mr. F. Mitchell. Photo by C. M. Cooke.

Ch. Singabeam Sheen of Gold, owned by Mr. A. A. Carter. Photo by C. M. Cooke.

there is a host of other drugs, new and old, that can also do the job efficiently. With most of the worm drugs, give no food to the dog for twenty-four hours, or in the case of puppies, twenty hours previous to the time he is given the medicine. It is absolutely essential that this starvation limit be adhered to, particularly if the drug used is tetrachlorethylene, since the existence of the slightest amount of food in the stomach or intestine can cause death. One tenth c.c. to each pound of the animal's weight is the dosage for tetrachlorethylene, followed in one hour by a milk-of-magnesia physic, never an oily physic. Food may be given two hours later.

N-butyl-chloride is less toxic if the dog has eaten some food during the supposed starvation period. The dosage is one c.c. for every ten pounds of the weight of the dog. Any safe physic may be administered an hour later, and the dog fed within two hours afterward. Large doses of this drug can be given grown dogs without danger and will kill whipworms as well as roundworms. A second treatment should follow in two weeks. The effect of N-butyl-chloride is cumulative;

therefore, when a large dosage is necessary, the total amount to be given can be divided into many small doses administered, one small dose at a time, over a period of hours. The object of this procedure is to prevent the dog from vomiting up the drug, which generally occurs when a large dose is given all at once. This method of administering the drug has been found to be very effective.

HOOKWORMS

These tiny leeches who live on the blood of your dog, which they get from the intestinal walls, cause severe anemia, groaning, fits, diarrhea, loss of appetite and weight, rapid breathing, and swelling of the legs. The same treatment used to eradicate roundworms will also expel hookworms.

Good food is essential for quick recovery, with added amounts of liver and raw meat incorporated in the diet. Blood transfusions are

Your veterinarian can immunize your Collie puppy against many of the diseases of puppyhood.

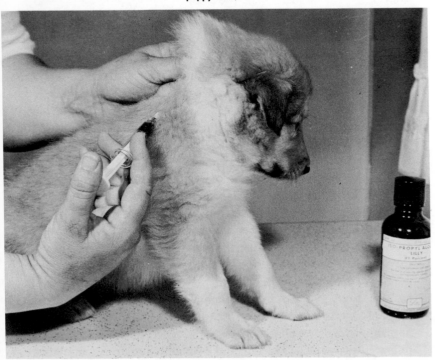

Ch. Mywicks Mylady Fair, owned by Mr. J. E. Mycroft. Photo by C. M. Cooke.

often necessary if the infestation has been heavy. If one infestation follows another, a certain degree of immunity to the effects of the parasite seems to be built up by the dog. A second treatment should be given two weeks following the initial treatment.

WHIPWORMS

These small, thin whiplike worms are found in the intestines and the caecum. Those found in the intestines are reached and killed by the same drugs used in the eradication of roundworms and hookworms. Most worm medicines will kill these helminths if they reach them, but those which live in the caecum are very difficult to reach. They exude toxins which cause debilitation, anemia, and allied ills, and are probably a contributing factor in lowering the resistance to the onslaught of other infections. The usual symptoms of worm infestation are present.

N-butyl-chloride, in dosage three times greater than the roundworm dosage, appears to be quite effective in reaching the caecum

Ch. Mywicks Meadow Lancer, owned by Mr. J. E. Mycroft. Photo by C. M. Cooke.

and ridding the dog of most of these pests. The drug is to be given following the twenty-four hour period of fasting. Administration of an anti-emetic is generally indicated to keep the dog from disgorging the drug.

Hydrogen peroxide, administered as an enema, is highly effective but very dangerous, and should be applied only by expert hands.

TAPEWORMS

Tapeworms are not easily diagnosed by fecal test, but are easily identified when visible in the dog's stool. The worm is composed of two distinct parts, the head and the segmented body. It is pieces of the segmented body that we see in the stools of the dog. They are usually flat and pink or white in color. The common tapeworm, which is most prevalent in our dogs, is about eighteen inches long, and the larvae are carried by the flea. The head of the worm is smaller than a pinhead and attaches itself to the intestinal wall. Contrary to general belief, the dog infested with tapeworms does not possess an enormous appetite—rather it fluctuates from good to poor. The animal shows the general signs of worm infestation. Often he squats and drags his hindquarters on the ground. This is due to tapeworm larvae moving and wriggling in the lower bowels. One must be careful in diagnosing this symptom, as it may also mean that the dog is suffering from distended anal glands.

Arecolene is an efficient expeller of tapeworms. Dosage is approximately one-tenth grain for every fifteen pounds of the dog's weight, administered after twenty hours of fasting. Nemural is also widely used. One pill for every eight pounds of body weight is given in a small amount of food after twelve hours of starvation. No worm medicine can be considered 100 per cent effective in all cases. If one drug does not expel the worms satisfactorily, then another must be tried.

Ch. Sandamac's Sandasue.

HEARTWORM

This villain inhabits the heart and is the most difficult to treat. The worm is about a foot long and literally stuffs the heart of the affected animal. It is prevalent in the southern states and has long been the curse of sporting-dog breeds. This does not signify that your Collie cannot become infected, since the worm is transmitted principally through the bite of an infected mosquito, which can fly from an infected southern canine visitor directly to your dog and do its dire deed.

The symptoms are: fatigue, gasping, coughing, nervousness, and sometimes dropsy and swelling of the extremities. Treatment for heartworms definitely must be left in the hands of your veterinarian. A wide variety of drugs are used in treatment; the most commonly employed are the arsenicals, antimony compounds, and caracide. Danger exists during cure when dying adult worms move to the lungs, causing suffocation, or when dead microfilariae, in a heavily infested dog, block the small blood vessels in the heart muscles. The invading microfilariae are not discernible in the blood until

If your Collie limps take him to the veterinarian immediately for an X-ray. Perhaps just an elastic supporting bandage is needed for the torn ligament.

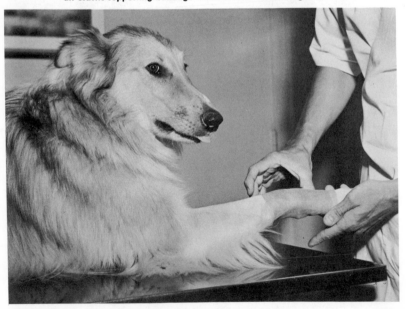

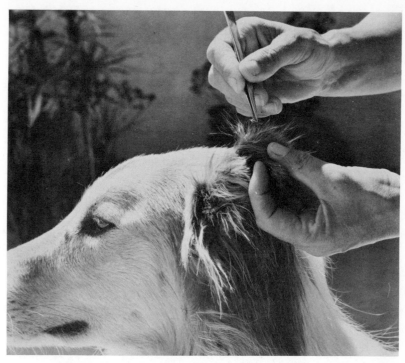

Burrs and insects can be picked from your Collie's coat with tweezers.

nine months following introduction of the disease by the bite of the carrier mosquito.

In an article on this subject in *Field and Stream* magazine, Joe Stetson describes a controlled experiment in which caracide was employed in periodic treatments as a preventive of heartworm. The experiment was carried out over a period of eighteen months, during which time the untreated dogs became positive for heartworm and eventually died. A post mortem proved the presence of the worm. The dogs that underwent scheduled prophylaxis have been found, by blood test, to be free of circulating microfilariae and are thriving.

COCCIDIOSIS

This disease is caused by a single-celled protozoa. It affects dogs of all ages but is not dangerous to mature animals. When puppies become infected by a severe case of coccidiosis, it very often proves fatal, since it produces such general weakness and emaciation that the puppy has no defense against other invading harmful organisms. Loose and bloody stools are indicative of the presence of this disease, as is loss of appetite, weakness, emaciation, discharge from the eyes, and a fever of approximately 103 degrees. The disease is contracted directly or through flies that have come from infected quarters. Infections seems to occur over and over again, limiting the puppy's chance of recovery with each succeeding infection. The duration of the disease is about three weeks, but new infestations can stretch this period of illness on until your puppy has little chance of recovery. Strict sanitation and supportive treatment of good nutrition—utiliz-

Older Collies also need 'shots' from time to time. It is really a painless process and the Collie, like children, is more afraid of the unknown than the treatment itself.

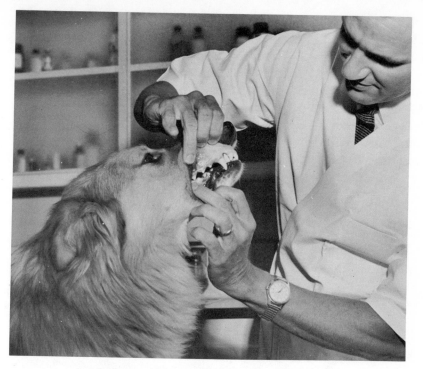

As a Collie gets older it begins to lose its teeth. This is normal.

ing milk, fat, kaopectate, and bone ash (a tablespoonful a day for Collie puppies), with added dextrose and calcium—seem to be all that can be done in the way of treatment. Force feed the puppy if necessary. The more food that you can get into him to give him strength until the disease has run its course, the better will be his chances of recovery. Specific cures have been developed in other animals and poultry, but not as yet in dogs. Recovered dogs are life-long carriers of the disease.

SKIN DISEASES

Diseases of the skin in dogs are many, varied, and easily confused by the kennel owner as to category. All skin afflictions should be immediately diagnosed by your veterinarian so that treatment can begin with dispatch. Whatever drug is prescribed must be employed diligently and in quantity and generally long after surface indications of the disease have ceased to exist. A surface cure may be attained,

Ch. Viscount Pilot, owned by Mr. A. E. Atack. Photo by C. M. Cooke.

but the infection remains buried deep in the hair follicles or skin glands, to erupt again if treatment is suspended too soon. Contrary to popular belief, diet, if well balanced and complete, is seldom the cause of skin disease.

Eczema

The word "eczema" is a much-abused word, as is the word "dermatitis." Both are used with extravagance in the identification of various forms of skin disorders. We will concern ourselves with the two most prevalent forms of so-called eczema, namely wet eczema and dry eczema. In the wet form, the skin exudes moisture and then scabs over, due to constant scratching and biting by the dog at the site of infection. The dry form manifests itself in dry patches which irritate and itch, causing great discomfort to the dog. In both instances the hair falls out and the spread of the disease is rapid. The cause of these diseases is not yet known, though many are thought to have originated from various fungi and aggravated by allergic conditions. The quickest means of bringing these diseases under control is through the application of a good skin remedy often combined with a fungicide, which your veterinarian will prescribe. An over-all dip, employing specific liquid medication, is beneficial in many cases and has a continuing curative effect over a period of days.

Ringworm

This infection is caused by a fungus and is highly contagious to humans. In the dog it generally appears on the face as a round or oval spot from which the hair has fallen. It is not as often seen in Collies as it is in shorter-coated dogs. Ringworm is easily cured by the application of iodine glycerine (50 per cent of each ingredient) or a fungicide liberally applied. The new antibiotic Malucidin eliminates ringworm quickly and effectively.

Acne

Your puppy will frequently display small eruptions on the soft skin of his belly. These little pimples rupture and form a scab.

Ch. Swintonian Model, owned by Mr. J. Franey. Photo by C. M. Cooke.

The rash is caused by inflammation of the skin glands and is not a serious condition. Treatment consists of washing the affected area with alcohol or witch hazel, followed by the application of a healing lotion or powder, such as B.F.I., or army formula foot powder, which is similar to Quinsana.

Hookworm Larvae Infection

The skin of your dog can become infected from the eggs and larvae of the hookworm acquired from muddy hookworm-infested runs. The larvae become stuck to his coat with mud and burrow into the skin, leaving ugly raw red patches. One or two baths in warm water to which an antiseptic has been added usually cures the condition quickly.

DEFICIENCY DISEASES

These diseases, or conditions, are caused by dietary deficiencies or some condition which robs the diet of necessary ingredients. Anemia, a deficiency condition, is a shortage of hemoglobin. Hookworms,

Ch. Accalia's Blue Aspiration.

Rock Dorburt Royal Heir, owned by Mrs. Herbert Bauman.

lice, and any disease that depletes the system of red blood cells, are contributory causes. A shortage or lack of specific minerals or vitamins in the diet can also cause anemia. Not so long ago, rickets was the most common of the deficiency diseases, caused by a lack of one or more of the dietary elements—vitamin D, calcium, and phosphorous. There are other types of defiency diseases originating in dietary inadequacy and characterized by unthriftiness in one or more phases. The cure exists in supplying the missing food factors to the diet. Sometimes, even though all the necessary dietary elements are present in the food, some are destroyed by improper feeding procedure. For example, a substance in raw eggs, avertin, destroys biotin, one of the B-complex group of vitamins. Cooking will destroy the avertin in the egg white and prevent a biotin deficiency in the diet.

BACTERIAL DISEASES

In this group we find leptospirosis, tetanus, pneumonia, strep infections, and many other dangerous diseases. The mortality rate is generally high in all of the bacterial diseases, and treatment should be left to your veterinarian.

Leptospirosis

Leptospirosis is spread most frequently by the urine of infected dogs, which can infect for six months or more after the ainmal has recovered from the disease. Rats are the carriers of the bacterial agent which produces this disease. A dog will find a bone upon

Ch. Glenhusset Superb, owned by Mr. R. Morris. Photo by C. M. Cooke.

Ch. Danvis Derna, owned by Mr. T. D. Purvis. Photo by C. M. Cooke.

which an infected rat has urinated, chew the bone, and become infested with the disease in turn. Leptospirosis is primarily dangerous in the damage it does to the kidneys. Complete isolation of affected individuals to keep the disease from spreading and rat control of kennel areas are the chief means of prevention. Also, newly developed vaccines may be employed by your veterinarian as a preventive measure. Initial diagnosis is difficult, and the disease has generally made drastic inroads before a cure is effected. It has been estimated that fully 50 per cent of all dogs throughout the world have been stricken with leptospirosis at one time or another and that in many instances the disease was not recognized for what it was. The disease produced by *Leptospira* in the blood of humans is known as Weil's disease.

Tetanus

Lockjaw bacteria produce an exceedingly deadly poison. The germs grow in the depths of a sealed-over wound where oxygen cannot penetrate. To prevent this disease, every deep wound acquired by your dog should be thoroughly cleansed and disinfected, and an antitoxin given the animal. Treatment follows the same general pattern as prevention. If the jaw locks, intravenous feeding must be given.

Strep throat

This is a very contagious disease caused by a specific group of bacteria labeled "streptococcus." Characteristic of this disease is the high temperature that accompanies infection (104 to 106 degrees). Other symptoms are loose stool at the beginning of the disease and a slight optic discharge. The throat becomes intensely inflamed, swallowing is difficult, and the glands under the ears are swollen. Immunity is developed by the host after the initial attack.

Tonsillitis

Inflammation of the tonsils can be of either bacterial or virus origin. It is not a serious disease in itself, but is often a symptom of other diseases. Tonsillitis is not to be confused with strep throat, which is produced by an entirely different organism. The symptoms of tonsilitis are enlarged and reddened tonsils, poor appetite, vomiting, and optic discharge. The disease usually runs its course in from five to seven days. Penicillin, aureomycin, terramycin, chloromycetin, etc., have been used with success in treatment.

Pneumonia

Pneumonia is a bacterial disease of the lungs of which the symptoms are poor appetite, optic discharge, shallow and rapid respiration. Affected animals become immune to the particular type of pneumonia from which they have recovered. Oral treatment utilizing antibiotic or sulfa drugs, combined with a pneumonia jacket of cloth or cotton padding wrapped around the chest area, seems to be standard treatment.

VIRUS DISEASES

The dread virus diseases are caused by the smallest organisms known to man. They live in the cells and often attack the nerve tissue. The tissue thus weakened is easily invaded by many types of bacteria. Complications then set in, and it is these accompanying ills which usually prove fatal. The secondary infections can be treated with several of the "wonder" drugs, and excellent care and nursing is necessary if the stricken animal is to survive. Your veterinarian is the only person qualified to aid your dog when a virus disease strikes. The diseases in this category include distemper, infectious hepatitis, rabies, kennel cough, housedog disease, and primary encephalitis—the latter actually inflammation of the brain, a condition characterizing several illnesses, particularly those of virus origin.

Distemper

Until recently a great many separate diseases had been lumped under the general heading of distemper.* In the last few years modern science has isolated a number of separate diseases of the distemper complex, such as infectious hepatitis, hard-pad disease, influenza, and primary encephalitis, which had been diagnosed as distemper. Thus, with more accurate diagnosis, great strides have been made in conquering not only distemper, but these other, allied diseases. Distemper (Carre) is no longer prevalent due to successful methods of immunization, but any signs of illness in an animal

*See L. F. and G. D. Whitney, *The Distemper Complex* (Jersey City, New Jersey, T.F.H. Pubs.).

Ch. Selstone Sequence, owned by Mr. T. E. Tomlinson. Photo by C. M. Cooke.

not immunized may be the beginning of the disease. The symptoms are so similar to those of various other diseases that only a trained observer can diagnose correctly. Treatment consists of the use of drugs to counteract complications arising from the invasion of secondary diseases and in keeping the stricken animal warm, well fed, comfortable and free from dehydration until the disease has run its course. In many instances, even if the dog gets well, he will be left with some dreadful souvenir of the disease which will mar him for life. Aftereffects are common in most of the diseases of the distemper complex.

The tremendous value of immunization against this virus disease cannot be exaggerated. Except for the natural resistance your animal carries against disease, it is the one means of protection you have against this killer. There have been various methods of immunization developed in the last several years, but it would seem that the most recently favored is the avianized vaccine (or chick embryo-adapted

Ch. Lovely Romance, owned by Mrs. L. A. Reed. Photo by C. M. Cooke.

Dunrobin Token o'Halmaric, owned by Mr. and Mrs. R. A. Engle. Photo by Anton Kamp.

vaccine). There are reasonably sure indications that this avianized vaccine protects against hard-pad disease and primary encephalitis as well as distemper. Injections can be given at any age, even as early as six or eight weeks, with a repeat dosage at six months of age. It does not affect the tissues, nor can it cause any ill effects to other dogs in a kennel who come in contact with the vaccinated animal.

Infectious hepatitis

This disease attacks dogs of all ages but is particularly deadly to puppies. We see young Collie puppies in the nest, healthy, bright and sturdy; suddenly they begin to vomit, and the next day they are dead of infectious hepatitis—it strikes that quickly. The disease is almost impossible to diagnose correctly and there is no known treatment that will cure it. Astute authorities claim that if an afflicted dog survives three days after the onslaught of the disease he will, in all probability, recover completely. Research is under way at present upon a vaccine that will afford safe and effective protection against infectious hepatitis.

Rabies

This is the most terrible of diseases, since it knows no bounds. It is transmissible to all kinds of animals and birds, including the superior animal, man. To contract this dread disease, the dog must be bitten by a rabid animal or the rabies virus must enter the body through a broken skin surface. The disease incubation period is governed by the distance of the virus point of entry to the brain. The closer the point of entry is to the brain, the quicker the disease manifests itself. We can be thankful that rabies is not nearly as prevalent as is supposed by the uninformed. Restlessness, excitability, perverted appetite, character reversal, wildness, drowsiness, loss of acuteness of senses, and of feeling in some instances, foaming at the mouth, and many other lesser symptoms come with the onslaught of this disease. Diagnosis by trained persons of a portion of the brain is conceded to be the only way of determining whether an animal died of rabies or of one of the distemper complex diseases. Very little has been done in introducing drugs or specifics that can give satisfaction in combating this disease; perhaps evaluation of the efficacy of such products is almost impossible with a disease so rare and so difficult to diagnose.

In 1948 an avianized, modified live virus vaccine was reported, and is being used in clinical trials with some success. Quarantine, such as that pursued in England, even of six-months duration, is still not the answer to the rabies question, though it is undeniably effective. It is, however, not proof positive. Recently a dog on arriving in England was held in quarantine for the usual six months. The day before he was to be released to his owners, the attendant noticed that he was acting strangely. He died the next day. Under examination his brain showed typical inclusion bodies, establishing the fact that he had died of rabies. This is a truly dangerous disease that can bring frightful death to animal or man. When an effective way of immunization is found and recommended by authoritative sources, it should be the duty of every dog owner to protect his dog, himself, his family, and neighbors from even the slight risk that exists of contracting rabies by taking immediate advantage of this form of protection.

FITS

Fits in dogs are symptoms of diseases rather than illness itself. They can be caused by the onslaught of any number of diseases, including worms, distemper, epilepsy, primary encephalitis, poisoning, etc. Running fits can also be traced to dietary deficiencies. The

Ch. Lovely Lady of Glenmist, owned by Mr. F. Mitchell. Photo by C. M. Cooke.

underlying reason for the fits, or convulsions, must be diagnosed by your veterinarian and the cause treated.

DIARRHEA

Diarrhea, which is officially defined as watery movements occuring eight or more times a day, is often a symptom of one of many other diseases. But if, on taking your Collie's temperature, you find there is no fever, it is quite possible the condition has been caused by either a change of diet, of climate or water, or even by a simple intestinal disturbance. A tightening agent such as kaopectate should be given. Water should be withheld and corn syrup, dissolved in boiled milk, substituted to prevent dehydration in the patient. Feed hard-boiled eggs, boiled milk, meat, cheese, boiled white rice, cracker, kibbles, or dog biscuits. Add a tablespoonful of bone ash (not bone meal) to the diet. If the condition is not corrected within two or

Windswept Renegade.

234

Ch. Antoc Tawny Tattoo, owned by Mrs. A. Speding. Photo by C. M. Cooke.

three days, if there is an excess of blood passed in the stool, or if signs of other illness become manifest, don't delay a trip to your veterinarian.

CONSTIPATION

If the dog's stool is so hard that it is difficult for him to pass it and he strains and grunts during the process, then he is obviously constipated. The cause of constipation is one of diet. Bones and dog biscuits, given abundantly, can cause this condition, as can any of the items of diet mentioned above as treatment for diarrhea. Chronic constipation can result in hemorrhoids which, if persistent, must be removed by surgery. The cure for constipation and its accompanying ills is the introduction of laxative food elements into the diet. Stewed tomatoes, buttermilk, skim milk, whey, bran, alfalfa meal, and various fruits can be fed and a bland physic given. Enemas can bring quick relief. Once the condition is rectified, the dog should be given a good balanced diet, avoiding all types of foods that will produce constipation.

EYE AILMENTS

The eyes are not only the mirror of the soul, they are also the mirror of many kinds of disease. Discharge from the eyes is one of the many symptoms warning of most internal virus, parasitic, and bacterial diseases. Of the ailments affecting the eye itself, the most usual are: glaucoma, which seems to be an hereditary disease; pink eye, a strep infection; cataracts; opacity of the lens in older dogs; corneal opacity, such as follows some cases of infectious hepatitis; and teratoma. Mange, fungus, inturned lids, and growths on the lid are other eye ailments. The wise procedure is to consult your veterinarian for specific treatment.

When the eyes show a discharge for reasons other than those that can be labeled "ailment," such as irritation from dust, wind, or sand, they should be washed with warm water on cotton or a soft cloth. After gently washing the eyes, an ophthalmic ointment combining a mild anesthetic and antiseptic can be utilized. Butyn sulphate, 1 per cent yellow oxide of mercury, and 5 per cent sulphathiazole ointment are all good. Boric acid seems to be falling out of favor as an ophthalmic antiseptic. The liquid discharged by the dog's tear ducts is a better antiseptic, and much cheaper.

ANAL GLANDS

If your dog consistently drags his rear parts on the ground or bites this area, the cause is probably impacted anal glands. These glands, which are located on each side of the anus, should be periodically cleared by squeezing. The job is not a nice one, and can be done much more effectively by your veterinarian. Unless these glands are kept reasonably clean, infection can become housed in this site, resulting in the formation of an abscess which will need surgical care. Dogs that get an abundance of exercise seldom need attention to the anal glands.

The many other ailments to which your dog is heir such as cancer, tumors, rupture, heart disease, fractures, and the results of accidents, etc., must all be diagnosed and tended to by your veterinarian. When you go to your veterinarian with a sick dog, always remember to bring along a sample of his stool for analysis. Many times samples of his urine are needed, too. Your veterinarian is the only one qualified to treat your dog for disease, but protection against disease is, to a great extent, in the hands of the dog's owner. If those hands are capable, a great deal of pain and misery for both dog and owner can be eliminated. Death can be cheated, investment saved, and veterinary bills kept to a minimum. A periodic health check by your veterinarian is a wise investment.

ADMINISTERING MEDICATION

Some people seem to have ten thumbs on each hand when they attempt to give medicine to their dog. They become agitated and approach the task with so little sureness that their mood is communicated to the patient, increasing the difficulties presented. Invite calmness and quietness in the patient by emanating these qualities yourself. Speak to the animal in low, easy tones, petting him slowly, quieting him down in preparation. The administration of medicine should be made without fuss and as though it is some quiet and private new game between you and your dog.

At the corner of your dog's mouth there is a lip pocket perfect for the administering of liquid medicine if used correctly. Have the

This is the proper way of muzzling a Collie that is suspected of being a biter.

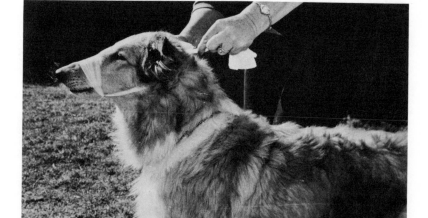

Collies are at their best when they are 'shepherding.'

animal sit, then raise his muzzle so that his head is slanted upward looking toward the sky. Slide two fingers in the corner of his mouth where the upper and lower lip edges join, pull gently outward, and you have a pocket between the cheek flesh and the gums. Into this pocket pour the liquid medicine at the rate of approximately two tablespoonfuls at a time for a full-grown Collie. Keep his head up, and the liquid will run from the pocket into his throat and he will swallow it. Continue this procedure until the complete dose has been given. This will be easier to accomplish if the medicine has been spooned into a small bottle. The bottle neck, inserted into the lip pocket, is tipped, and the contents drained at the ratio mentioned above.

To give pills or capsules, the head of the patient must be raised with muzzle pointing upward. With one hand, grasp the cheeks of the dog just behind the lip edges where the teeth come together on the inside of the mouth. With the thumb on one side and the fingers on the other, press inward as though squeezing. The lips are pushed against the teeth, and the pressure of your fingers forces the mouth open. The dog will not completely close his mouth, since doing so

Ch. Peterblue Jaunty, owned by Mrs. M. Castle. Photo by C. M. Cooke.

would cause him to bite his lips. With your other hand, insert the pill in the patient's mouth as far back on the base of the tongue as you can, pushing it back with your second finger. Withdraw your hand quickly, allow the dog to close his mouth, and hold it closed with your hand, but not too tightly. Massage the dog's throat and watch for the tip of his tongue to show between his front teeth, signifying the fact that the capsule or pill has been swallowed.

In taking your dog's temperature, an ordinary rectal thermometer is adequate. It must be first shaken down, then dipped in vaseline, and inserted into the rectum for approximately three-quarters of its length. Allow it to remain there for no less than a full minute, restraining the dog from sitting completely during that time. When withdrawn, it should be wiped with a piece of cotton, read, then washed in alcohol—never hot water. The arrow on most thermometers at 98.6 degrees indicates normal human temperature and should be disregarded. Normal temperature for your grown dog is 101 degrees; normal puppy temperature varies between $101\frac{1}{2}$ and 102 degrees. Excitement can raise the temperature, so it is best to take a reading only after the dog is calm.

In applying an ophthalmic ointment to the eye, simply pull the lower lid out, squeeze a small amount of ointment into the pocket thus produced, and release the lid. The dog will blink, and the ointment will spread over the eye.

Should you find it necessary to give your dog an enema, employ an ordinary human-size bag and rubber hose. For a Collie a catheter is not necessary. Simply grease the rubber hose tip with vaseline and insert the hose well into the rectum. The bag should be held high for a constant flow of water. A quart of warm soapy water or plain water with a tablespoonful of salt makes an efficient enema.

Ch. Selskars Peterblue Susan, owned by Mrs. J. E. Hill. Photo by C. M. Cooke.

Ch. Jefsfire Strollaway, owned by Mr. and Mrs. A. T. Jeffries. Photo by C. M. Cooke.

FIRST AID

Emergencies quite frequently occur which make it necessary for you to care for the dog yourself until veterinary aid is available. Quite often emergency help by the owner can save the dog's life or lessen the chance of permanent injury. A badly injured animal, blinded to all else but abysmal pain, often reverts to the primitive wanting only to be left alone with his misery. Injured, panic-stricken, not recognizing you, he might attempt to bite when you wish to help him. Under the stress of fright and pain, this reaction is normal in animals. A muzzle can easily be slipped over his fore-face, or a piece of bandage or strip of cloth can be fashioned into a muzzle by looping it around the dog's muzzle, crossing it under the jaws, and bringing the two ends around in back of the dog's head and tying them. Snap a leash onto his collar as quickly as possible to prevent him from running away and hiding. If it is necessary to lift him, grasp him by the neck, getting as large a handful of skin as you can, as high up on the neck as possible. Hold tight and he won't be able to turn his head far enough around to bite. Lift him by the hold you have on his neck until he is far enough off the ground to enable you to encircle his body with your other arm and support him or carry him.

Every dog owner should have handy a first-aid kit specifically for the use of his dog. It should contain a thermometer, surgical scissors, rolls of three-inch and six-inch bandage, a roll of one-inch adhesive tape, a package of surgical cotton, a jar of vaseline, enema equipment, bulb syringe, ten c.c. hypodermic syringe, flea powder, skin remedy, tweezers, ophthalmic ointment, paregoric, kaopectate, peroxide of hydrogen, merthiolate, army formula foot powder, alcohol, are remedy, aspirin, milk of magnesia, castor oil, mineral oil, dressing salve.

We have prepared two charts for your reference, one covering general first-aid measures and the other a chart of poisons and antidotes. Remember that, in most instances, these are emergency measures, not specific treatments, and are designed to help you in aiding your dog until you can reach your veterinarian.

FIRST-AID CHART

Emergency	Treatment	Remarks
Accidents	Automobile, Treat for shock. If gums are white, indicates probable internal injury. Wrap bandage tightly around body until it forms a sheath. Keep very quiet until veterinarian comes.	Call veterinarian immediately.
Bee stings	Give paregoric, 2 teaspoonsful for grown Collie, or aspirin to ease pain. If in state of shock, treat for same.	Call veterinarian for advice.
Bites (animal)	Tooth wounds—area should be shaved and antiseptic solution flowed into punctures with eye dropper. Iodine, merthiolate, etc., can be used. If badly bitten or ripped, take dog to your veterinarian for treatment.	If superficial wounds become infected after first aid, consult veterinarian.
Bloat	Stomach distends like a balloon. Pierce stomach wall with hollow needle to allow gas to escape. Follow with stimulant—2 cups of coffee. Then treat for shock.	

Burns	Apply strong, strained tea to burned area, followed by covering of vaseline.	Unless burn is very minor, consult veterinarian immediately.
Broken bones	If break involves a limb, fashion splint to keep immobile. If ribs, pelvis, shoulder, or back involved, keep dog from moving until professional help comes.	Call veterinarian immediately.
Choking	If bone, wood, or any foreign object can be seen at back of mouth or throat, remove with fingers. If object can't be removed or is too deeply imbedded or too far back in throat, rush to veterinarian immediately.	
Cuts	Minor cuts: allow dog to lick and cleanse. If not within his reach, clean cut with peroxide, then apply merthiolate. Severe cuts: apply pressure bandage to stop bleeding—a wad of bandage over wound and bandage wrapped tightly over it. Take to veterinarian.	If cut becomes infected or needs suturing, consult veterinarian. (*see* TETANUS).
Dislocations	Keep dog quiet and take to veterinarian at once.	
Drowning	Artificial respiration. Lay dog on his side, push with hand on his ribs, release quickly. Repeat every 2 seconds. Treat for shock.	New method of artificial respiration as employed by fire department useful here.
Electric shock	Artificial respiration. Treat for shock.	Call veterinarian immediately.
Heat stroke	Quickly immerse the dog in cold water until relief is given. Give cold water enema. Or lay dog flat and pour cold water over him, turn electric fan on him, and continue pouring cold water as it evaporates.	Cold towel pressed against abdomen aids in reducing temp. quickly if quantity of water not available.
Porcupine quills	Tie dog up, hold him between knees, and pull all quills out with pliers. Don't forget tongue and inside of mouth.	See veterinarian to remove quills too deeply imbedded.
Shock	Cover dog with blanket. Administer stimulant (coffee with sugar). Allow him to rest, and soothe with voice and hand.	Alcoholic beverages are NOT a stimulant.
Snake bite	Cut deep X over fang marks. Drop potassium-permanganate into cut. Apply tourniquet above bite if on foot or leg.	Apply first aid only if a veterinarian or a doctor can't be reached.

Ch. Sheildon Sequin, owned by Mr. A. E. Atack. Photo by C. M. Cooke.

POISON	HOUSEHOLD ANTIDOTE
ACIDS	Bicarbonate of soda
ALKALIES	Vinegar or lemon juice
(cleansing agents)	
ARSENIC	Epsom salts
HYDROCYANIC ACID	Dextrose or corn syrup
(wild cherry; laurel leaves)	
LEAD	Epsom salts
(paint pigments)	
PHOSPHORUS	Peroxide of hydrogen
(rat poison)	
MERCURY	Eggs and milk
THEOBROMINE	Phenobarbital
(cooking chocolate)	
THALLIUM	Table salt in water
(bug poisons)	
FOOD POISONING	Peroxide of hydrogen, followed by enema
(garbage, etc.)	
STRYCHNINE	Sedatives, Phenobarbital, Nembutal.
DDT	Peroxide and enema

The important thing to remember when your Collie is poisoned is that prompt action is imperative. Administer an emetic immediately. Mix hydrogen peroxide and water in equal parts. Force eight to ten tablespoonfuls of this mixture down your dog, or up to twelve tablespoonfuls (this dosage for a fully grown Collie). In a few minutes he will regurgitate his stomach contents. Once this has been accomplished, call your veterinarian. If you know the source of the poison and the container from which it came is handy, you will find the antidote on the label. Your veterinarian will prescribe specific drugs and advise on their use.

The symptoms of poisoning include trembling, panting, intestinal pain, vomiting, slimy secretion from mouth, convulsions, coma. All these symptoms are also prevalent in other illnesses, but if they appear and investigation leads you to believe that they are the result of poisoning, act with dispatch as described.

Ch. Peterblue Scallop, owned by Mrs. K. M. Renton. Photo by C. M. Cooke.

15.
The Future

What does the future hold for our breed? We are not seers so we cannot predict the future. We can only review what has gone before and refrain from repeating the mistakes of the past or present and so find advancement in the time to come.

In the final analysis the future of the Collie is up to you, the owners and breeders. You must carry the responsibility for molding the future of the breed. New theories, new techniques, new discoveries are constantly being made in the many fields of scientific endeavor. Never-ending research uncovers new concepts in canine medicine, nutrition, physiology, psychology and genetics. Immunities and cures, now in the process of development, will destroy diseases

Ch. Ugony's Golden Gloria, owned by Miss D. M. Young. Photo by C. M. Cooke.

that today take a terrible toll. Under the microscope and in the testing kennel old problems are being met and defeated. Geneticists probe ever deeper into the why of being, giving us, if we will look for them, new answers to our breeding problems. We must face this future with open minds and with tolerance. We must learn to understand new concepts and avoid harking back blindly to the incomplete knowledge of the past. It is then our job to take the new tools we have been given to work with and use them well.

In you, the breeder, is vested the power to fashion heredity, to mold life, in this Collie breed. Yes, you can use this power that creates life and change, that brings special life-forms into being. You can design this pattern of heredity. To do so you must be aware of the power you have, and have the intelligence to use it well. If the future is to give us those things which we want for our breed, then we must clear our minds of inaccuracy and absorb truth instead. This is the future; a time when yesterday's miracles become today's facts.

So we come to the last page of our book, the last sentence, the last word. Yet, we do not feel that this should be labeled "The End," for beyond the last word that we write lie the many new words the future will write, continuing and improving on what you have read here. No, we will not call this "The End." Let us instead, borrow the title of our first chapter, and anticipating that which lies before us in the future, name this just . . .

THE BEGINNING

OUR DOG BOOKS
HAVE THE ANSWERS!

When you have a question that concerns your dog's health or well-being or your own enjoyment of him as a well-trained, responsive companion, you need authoritative, practical answers. . . and you need them fast.

H-962 LEW BURKE'S DOG TRAIN-ING. You can't train a dog until you know what makes him tick, and in this immensely interesting and highly illustrated point-by-point coverage of the art of training dogs premier expert Lew Burke makes it easy to train a dog (for general obedience, for guard duty, for simple and advanced tricks, for housebreaking) through the application of easily learned rules. Dog-owners who have become satisfied with less than the best from their dog in terms of obedience will be delighted by the results they'll achieve from applying Lew Burke's easily learned, easily applied advice. 32 pages of step-by-step color photos illustrating training techniques in addition to many pertinent and useful black and white photos. 256 pages; $9.95.

H-934 DOG OWNER'S ENCYCLO-PEDIA OF VETERINARY MEDICINE by Dr. Allan Hart. Here is a book that will become, next to his pet itself, the truest friend a dog-owner has. Page after page and chapter after chapter of valuable, pertinent information that allows an owner to make sure that his pet is given the best of care at all times. Easy to read yet brilliantly informative this big book is a must. 186 pages; $9.95.

H-927 ENCYCLOPEDIA OF DOG BREEDS, by Ernest H. Hart. This is the most complete all-breed dog book ever written. Every recognized breed as well as many that are virtually unknown in America is illustrated and discussed. The book contains six large color sections and a wealth of black and white photos and line drawings. History, management and care of all dogs is included along with new and fascinating breed information. 783 pages; $12.95.

Visit your pet shop today or write for a complete book list of all T.F.H. books about dogs and other pets.
T.F.H. PUBLICATIONS, Inc.
P.O. Box 27
Neptune City, NJ 07753

INDEX